PAINTING WITH

PASTELS, WAX, GOUACHE, COLLAGE...

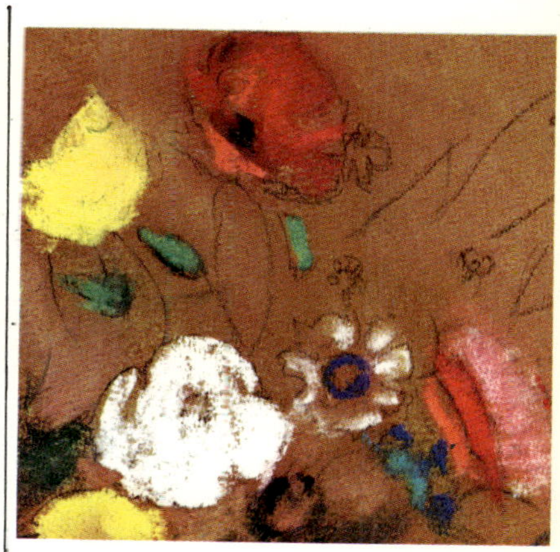

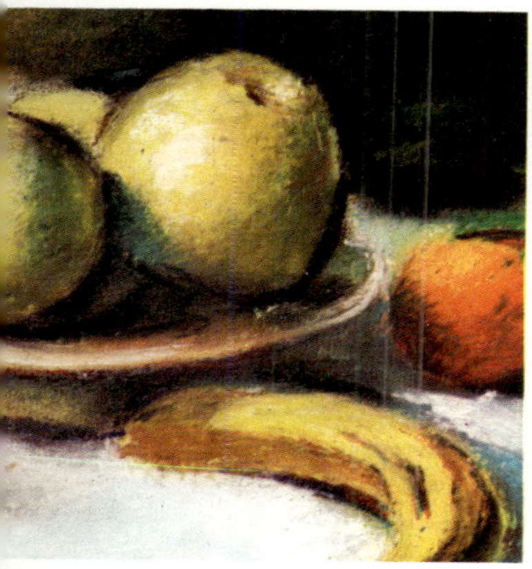

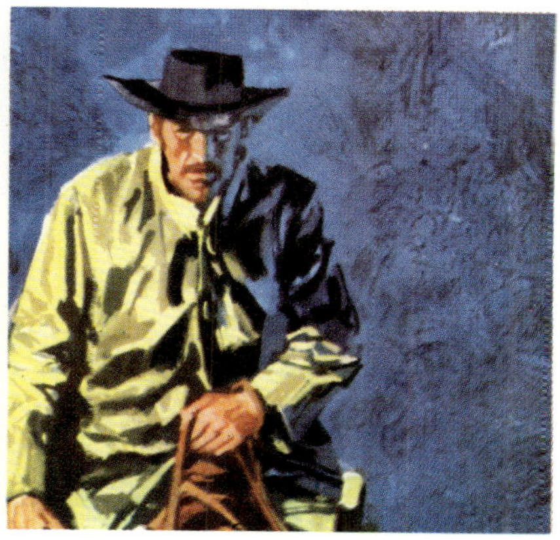

JOSE M. PARRAMON

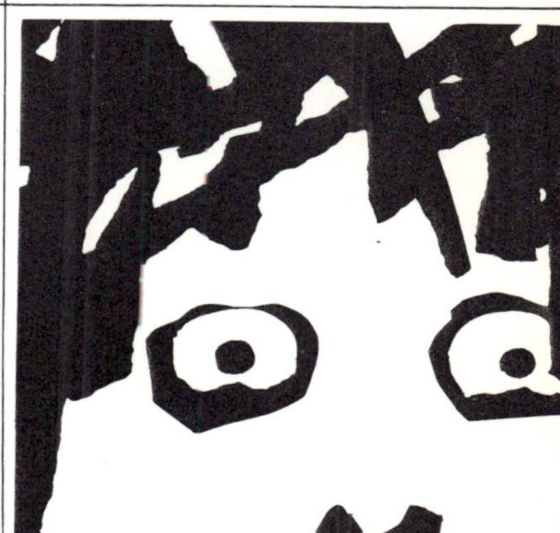

Parramón editions

Published by Parramón Ediciones, S.A.
Lepanto, 264 - 4.° - Barcelona - (Spain)
First edition, May 1984

Register Book Number: 785
Legal Deposit: B.18.111
ISBN.: 0 86343 0465

Printed in Spain by ALVAGRAF
Gerona, 6 - La Llagosta—
Barcelona

Distributed in the United Kingdom by
FOUNTAIN PRESS LTD.
65, Victoria Street,
Windsor, Berkshire SL41EH

'Painting and Drawing' Series

Distributors in U. K.

FOUNTAIN PRESS LTD.
65, Victoria Street, Windsor, Berkshire SL4 1EH
Telephone: Windsor 56959

CONTENTS

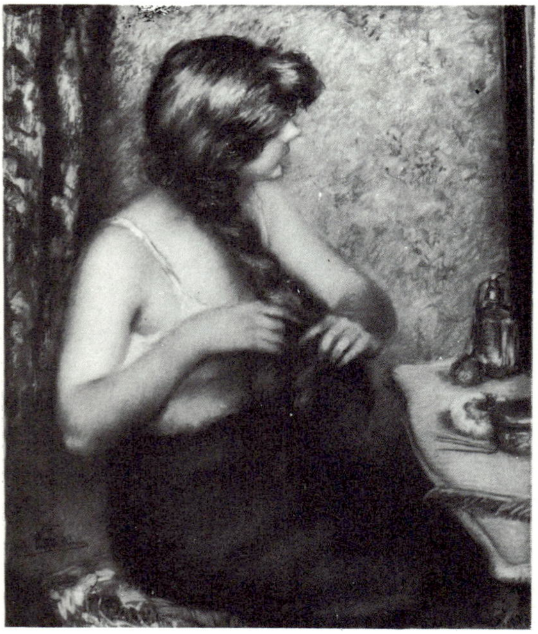

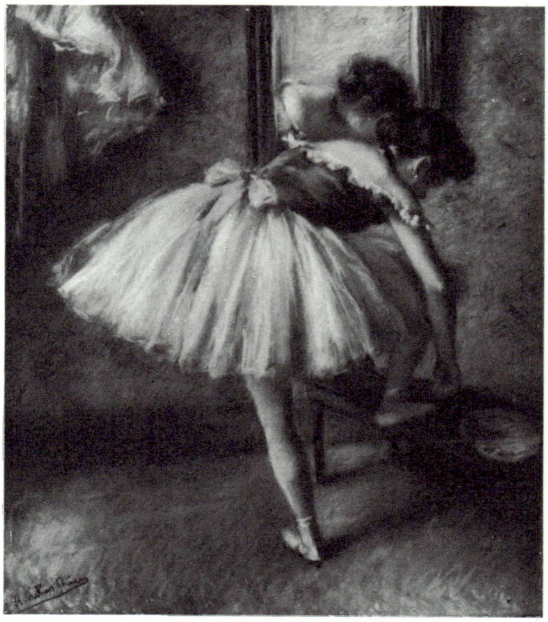

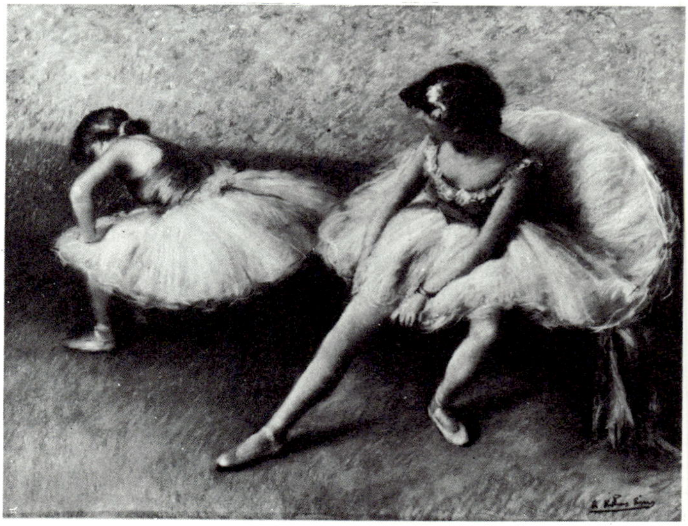

INTRODUCTION

This book combines the study and practice of various methods of painting and expression: pastel, wax and gouache or tempera painting, collage and monotype.

I honestly believe that this new book is an absolute "must" for a series devoted to teaching drawing and painting. I have had long experience in teaching these techniques and processes to pupils who have not used pastel, don't know about colours in gouache or tempera, and have never heard of monotype. I have proved that such study opened for them an amazing potential of expression, enriched their creative imagination and made them feel more capable afterwards of achieving one of those "sensational discoveries", as a good pupil and friend of mine called them. He was a doctor by profession and an amateur painter, and said, "The little you told me about monotype technique was a sensational discovery as far as I was concerned, and I set about creating monotypes for all I was worth. I feel like a painter, a lithographer, an artist! I have finished four already and I mean to do some more. It's really exciting!"

And so it is; and so is pastel painting, with its vigour and delicacy combined, as shown by Degas or Redon.

I think such a book must be appreciated through its making clear the little-known techniques of painting which offer extraordinary artistic potential. It was produced with the help of three famous artists, authors and advisers in the special techniques of pastel, collage and monotype respectively: Ramón Ribas Rius, José Plá Narbona and Enrique Huguet Muixí. I offer them my hearty thanks for their highly valued contribution.

This isn't a book just to be read, but to be "worked through"; one which calls upon the reader to create, paint in pastel, paint with colours in wax and practise and paint in gouache or tempera. It is a book for "Learning as you work".

J. M. Parramón

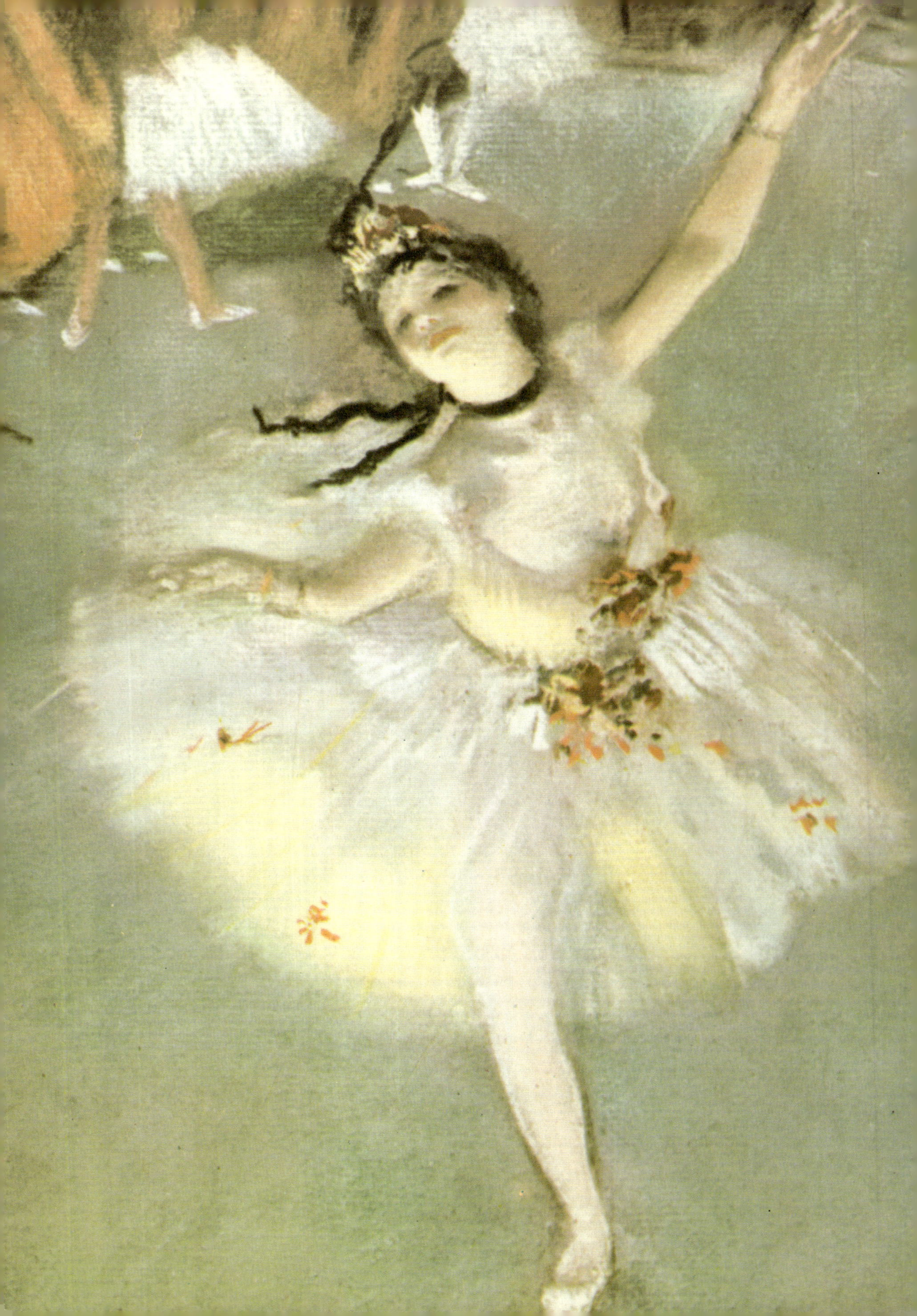

PASTELS

COLOURING WITH PASTELS

Pastels are made from earths, pigments, oils and resin

The basic constituents of pastels are powdered earth mixed with pigments and ground with oils, water and gummy substances. From these, a fairly solid mass is formed, to be made into the cylindrical shapes of pastel colours.

Pastel cannot be fixed

These sticks are extremely fragile — not surprising when you realise that they are simply a mixture of dust made to adhere to paper. Pastels can be scraped off paper with a finger. Furthermore, and this is a drawback, pastels cannot be fixed and made stable.

Yet the scope of pastel work is fascinating and wide. One can achieve marvellous subtleties and the brilliance and freshness of the colours stay bright and beautiful. When award-winning Spanish painter, Ribas Rius, was asked about his preference for pastels over oils, he answered that pastel work allowed him to achieve that instant clarity which is so difficult with oils, especially modern oil paints which are contaminated with artificial chemicals. Pastel, he said, has an unequalled clarity. The journalist who did the interview wrote that there should be no doubt as to the pastel's lasting qualities. Ribas Rius owns a reproduction of de La Tour's *Madame La Pompadour,* painted about two hundred years ago. The original hangs in the Louvre and its colouring is as alive today as it must have been the day it was finished.

Presentation: in cases holding 12 to 48 separate colours

Pastels are bought in cylindrical sticks, wrapped carefully in paper and labelled with the colour's name and reference number, making it simple to replace depleted stocks. Boxes of pastels are readily available with selections containing assortments of 12, 18, 24, 36 and 48 colours providing a huge range of blues, reds, yellows, greens and so on. This allows the artist to work without much blending of colours — we'll go into the mixing technique later. Cases were traditionally made of wood, but now pastels may be sold carefully wrapped in cotton wool in cardboard boxes.*

There are three gradations in pastel crayons: soft, normal and hard. Soft pastels are the popular choice and the only grade sold extensively by U.K. retailers. There are many makes – Rowney, Faber, Schminke (USA), Conté à Paris, Lefranc – all good names. The Otello company produce pastel-pencils, but professionals hardly ever use these.

Brands

Potential

Pastel shades have enormous artistic potential. They have been used in limitless ways, but, in particular, for portraits and for flowers. The medium was extremely fashionable in the eighteenth century, with such leading exponents as Greuze, de La Tour and Boucher. British painters such as Francis Cotes were popular, followed by Russell, Lawrence and others. Pastels came back into favour at the turn of the last century when they were used by some of the famous Impressionists, particularly Degas, with his ballet paintings and studies of the female nude. Other well-known artists favouring this medium were Toulouse-Lautrec (with his sketches from the Moulin Rouge), Renoir, Manet and Matisse. Pastels are very useful for the small-scale colour composition to be used as a guide for an oil painting. Commercial artists combine pastels with charcoal, Indian ink or pencil for figure sketches and also for final illustrations. US artist Charles Kingham's book, *Rendering Techniques,* shows how useful this medium can be in commercial art.

Paper

Textured Ingres paper can be bought in shades of cream, yellow, ochre, pink, dark green, blue and grey; this paper is a favourite of the pastel painter and Degas used it frequently. Another good surface for pastels is a shaded, slightly textured paper to which the pastel dust is held more firmly by small fibres, giving a more permanent result. Another special paper has a chamois leather type surface to which pastel adheres very firmly (and this means tricky corrections). Ordinary canvas can be used, too, and so can almost any paper with a rough surface, for example, a kind of wrapping paper, straw paper. And — this is important — for the artist's final painting — he will need a stiff surface, i.e. paper on cardboard or plywood, to give the necessary rigidity.

Use a stiff surface

* Geo Rowney & Co. Ltd, manufacturers of soft pastels, produce sets in wooden and cardboard boxes

HOW TO WORK WITH PASTELS

Rius' studio

Among leading exponents of pastel painting is the Spanish artist Ribas Rius. His studio in Barcelona is fit for a stage setting of La Bohème. It's old and roomy with a high ceiling and it's stacked with sketches and half-finished paintings. There is a low-cushioned sofa, an armchair, a few pictures and framed photographs on the walls. Everything is covered with fine grey dust from pastel-impregnated hands, paper and pastel holders. Part of a table is fitted out as a tray containing boxes of pastels — dozens of sticks and hundreds of bits of pastel sticks, some with flattened ends, some pointed, some very worn. This is the pastel painter's palette and here sits Rius with his easel. His model is posing against an old and stained canvas. She is dressed like a classical ballerina — in pure white.

Need for an easel

Rius is preparing to start painting. On the easel is a wooden board covered with light yellow straw paper. Rius first studies the subject and makes a charcoal sketch. He boxes up, estimates the play of light and shade and analyses the pose and the contrasts. He has, in fact, studied his pose long before, and has drawn a real ballerina in the wings of Barcelona's famous theatre. The theatre has a ballet company and Rius is often to be found there in the wings, sketch pad and pencil at the ready. This is where his pictures begin, with swift sketches of a ballerina fastening her shoe, perhaps, or adjusting her tutu. Back in his studio Rius studies each sketch and colours the most promising in tempera. Once he has chosen his subject (this may take a few days) he paints the final picture, using a model posing as far as possible as in his sketch. The sketch is essential because a professional model can't pose exactly as a ballerina would — the ballerina has very special posture and bearing, a particular way of bending and of stretching out her arm.

Starting your pastel

It's vital to have a sketch to give the sense of naturalness and get away from the model's artificial pose.

Charcoal sketch using a model

Rius spent two hours at this first sitting, using just charcoal. The model changed and left, having arranged the next sitting. Rius, however, continued his charcoal sketch; working without a model, he compares the two sketches — the real ballerina and the model — and changes the position of a foot and touches up a hand here and there.

Left: A Rius sketch from life, drawn in the theatre.
Right: one of his sketches coloured and finished off in the studio.

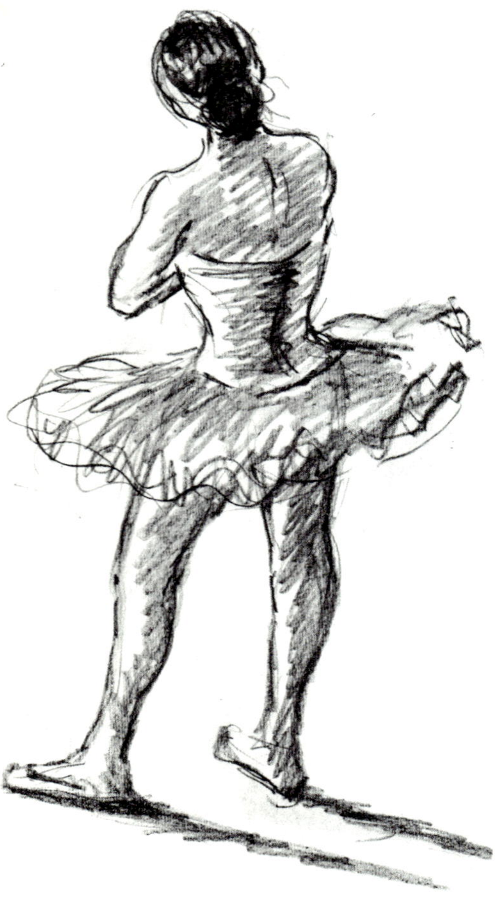

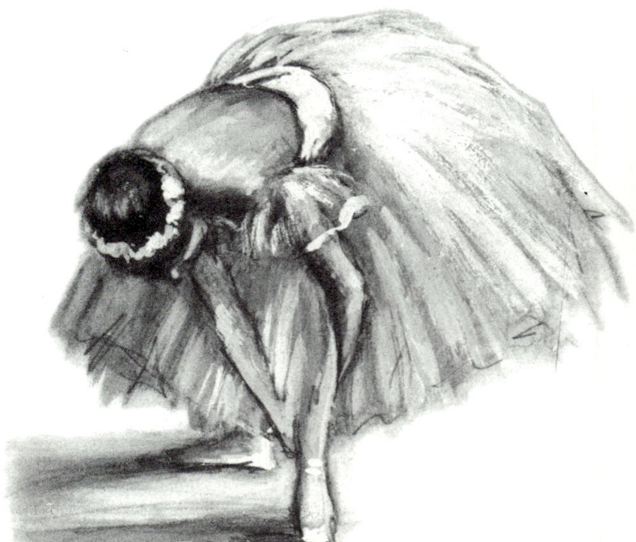

Tracing the sketch

Using tracing paper backed with charcoal, Rius transfers the study onto the final sheet which has been mounted on pasteboard. Then, with a medium charcoal pencil he alters the painting, changing a line here and there, concentrating on shading until the picture is ready for the pastel colouring. Next day the model comes back for another session. Rius has the final, grey-blue paper mounted on cardboard. He still uses the charcoal sketch for reference and explains its importance: sometimes he decides to draw in fairly free style, possibly not perfectly accurate, but just what is needed to help the final painting along.

Fragments of pastel

Rius can now start painting. He always uses fragments of pastel — never entire sticks. With pastel held between thumb and index and second fingers, he paints with the side of the pastel or uses the edge, depending whether he wants to get a patch of colour, a wide area or a smaller section. For drawing thin lines and delicate strokes he uses the piece of pastel like a pencil, taking a pointed edge and drawing with ease and fluency. He holds bits of colour in his left hand and continues painting with his right, changing and shading, combining colours all the time and using new colours from his palette.

Figs. A, B and C demonstrate the method of holding the pastel. You'll see that you need to paint with part of a stick, holding it with thumb and first and second fingers. Using just one end of the stump allows you to paint and graduate light and shade at the same time.

B

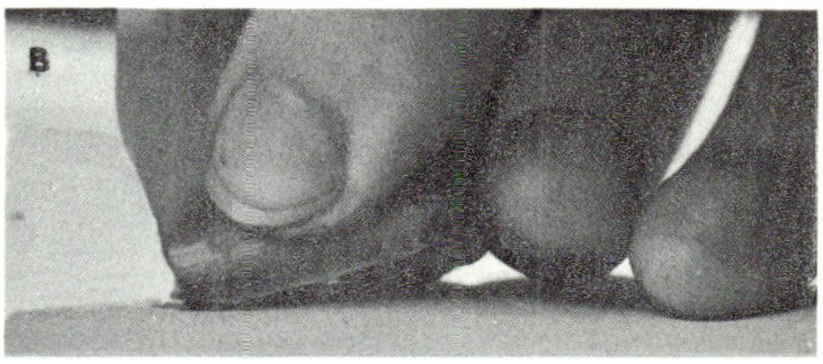

FIG. A

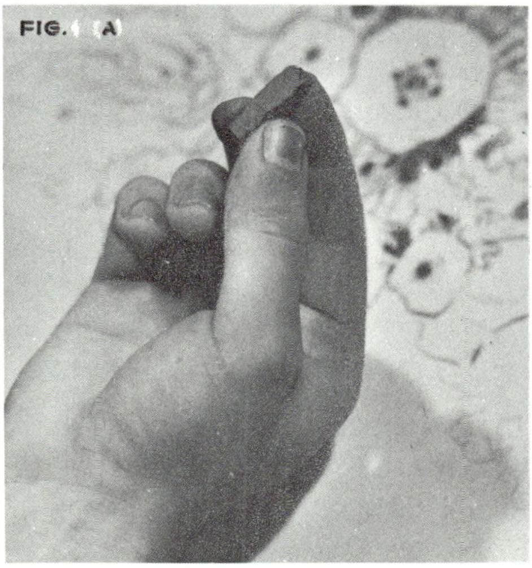

C

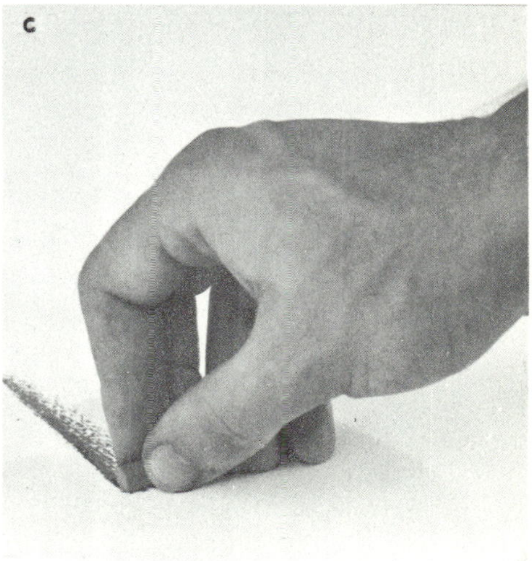

Rius paints the tutu, the flimsy white tulle skirt. Pastel has good covering properties and can be used in light colours on a darker background. He paints white on the grey surface, first using the pastel flat for a few touches and then toning down with a finger.

Shading with the fingers

A paper stump is not used in this technique. Fingers are much better for shading. To some extent they also fix the pastel: it contains greasy substances which help bind the powder; fingers are slightly greasy with perspiration, so in shading with the fingers and flattening the powder against the paper we are in some ways repeating the grinding and binding the pastel.

So this is Rius' advice — use fingers, not stumps. But this needs care; it's only too easy to overdo the shading. If the work is toned down too much it simply becomes dull and that's that.

Success with pastel involves the shading down of some parts and the use of the point for other sections.

Try to paint without mixtures

You'll sometimes need to draw over the shaded parts with the appropriate colour. Avoid mixtures as far as possible.

Working as described above should achieve pastel's typical quality of freshness — clean paint. The drawing can be appreciated and the patch of colour will look mint new. You will also get that doughy, slightly greasy effect which distinguishes this medium. Remember that pastel can be applied really thickly when needed, giving true density of colour. For example, when you paint a small patch of colour — a tiny flower, perhaps — and you make it with a single strong touch of pastel, you can pile on the substance to get an effect like the thick brush stroke in oil painting. But you won't get this effect by mixing colours. To get orange, for example, you mix yellow and red, first applying the yellow thickly. But when you put the red on top, the yellow is loosened, and comes off on your stick. You'll get your orange all right, but the mixing and flattening of the colours reduces the thickness and tends to lose that delicacy so typical of pastel. So you do need a good assortment of colours — boxes of as many as thirty-six or even forty-eight different colours.

Rius prepares to paint a bluish reflected light on the model's skirt. He needs to pick exactly the right shade — the choice is wide. There are dark, medium and light ultramarine, light and dark turquoise, Prussian blue, cobalt, sky blue, a bluish white shade, a violet-tinted white and another slightly darker tone. He selects the last shade and draws directly onto his paper, filling spaces with broad, powerful strokes, without any colour mixing.

Eighteen colours is the minimum

Eighteen colours is really the minimum for pastel painting. You'll need a greater assortment if you specialize in pastel.

Getting rid of surplus powder

Rius continues to paint. From time to time he puts down his pastel, taking the cardboard from his easel, setting it up on end and giving it a few light taps to blow away the surplus powder which remains on the surface without properly adhering to it. This is the reason for mounting your paper on cardboard — you need a solid edge to tap off the powder without damaging the paper.

Erasing — use a soft clean cloth

At this stage it's apparent that Rius has seen something wrong. A hand isn't quite right and it looks as if he's going to erase it. Using a clean piece of porous cloth he rubs gently on the offending hand, thinning the layers of pastel and leaving only a pale, faint coating. He paints over this quickly and easily. This is the way to erase pastel — indiarubbers make a mess —. A clean cloth id ideal.

Rius answered very definitely when I asked him if there was no liquid which could make pastel stick?

Pastel can't be fixed

"Yes, there's stuff for fixing it all right, but there's nothing to make it stick properly without altering the texture and the colour. Fixative is a liquid which, when sprayed, dampens the pastel. This encourages artificial masses of powder in the form of tiny clots which considerably alter the quality of the medium — that delicate floury patina of pastel. Moreover, fixative contains resinous substances which act as a varnish, moisten and change the colours and make them noticeably darker. Some brands of foreign fixatives, for example Talens made in the Netherlands, have achieved some substances which act as a varnish, moistening and changing the colours and making them noticeably deeper. Pastels by de La Tour, Degas and Redon in the Louvre and its annexe, the Jeu de Paume (devoted to the Impressionists), have maintained that lovely original brilliance. They have not been fixed and one could remove the whole work with a brush of one's hand.

Special framing

This is the reason for framing pastels with a space between the painting and the glass; glass is absolutely indispensable for pastels.

Rius has finished his session and the model will return the next day. The painter now spends some time just looking at this painting and will return in the evening to study it further with a fresh eye, so that next session another pastel painting will have been completed. But the final session is a difficult one. In this last stage, too much retouching and over-finishing can simply ruin a painting, changing it from something genuine and talented into a lifeless, affected picture. There has to be a moment when the painter says to himself: "That's enough!" This moment of truth comes with experience — it needs practice over the years.

PASTEL TECHNIQUE: A SUMMARY

1. For pastel painting you need a rigid surface and an easel.
2. Pastel is a medium with which you can overlay light colours on dark colours or backgrounds.
3. For broad strokes, hold the piece of pastel between your thumb and first and second fingers. For finer lines, hold it like a pencil.
4. For erasing or re-working a section, use a piece of old, clean cotton cloth.
5. Try to get a slightly misty effect with some direct strokes but plenty of shading.
6. Use fingers for shading.
7. You can mix two or more colours by shading or painting one on top of another.
8. However, try to paint with the tones of the draft sketch, without mixing colours.
9. You will need at least eighteen colours; for more specialized and detailed work you need many more.
10. Remember to shake off surplus powder now and again.
11. Pastel is difficult to fix. Framing and glazing is an absolute must. There must be a gap between the painting and the glass.

EXERCISE IN PASTELS

PAINTING A COPY OF REDON'S "WILD FLOWERS IN A LONG-NECKED VASE"

YOU WILL NEED: BOX OF EIGHTEEN PASTELS; SANGUINE CRAYON (is usually available as a Conté crayon in the U.K.); CHARCOAL PENCIL; A SOFT PENCIL; COTTON CLOTHS; RUBBER; RULER; SET-SQUARE; THICK CARD-BOARD (34×48 CM); YELLOW OCHRE INGRES PAPER; THIN TRACING PAPER; FIXATIVE.

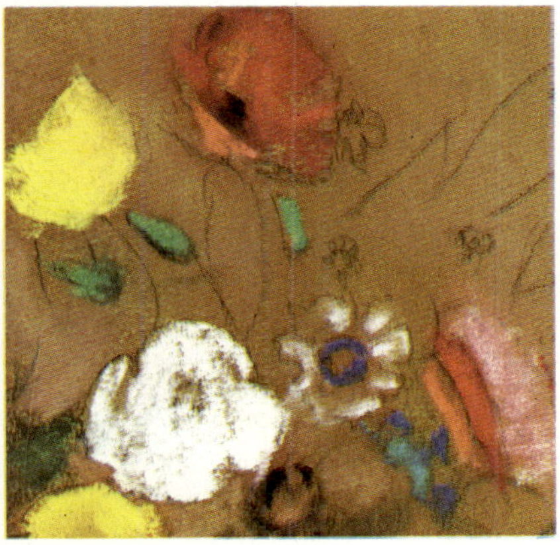

As usual, you learn as you go along, studying the technique and using your pastels. For this exercise we shall copy a picture from an art gallery: the French Impressionist Odilon Redon's painting of flowers in a long-necked vase. It hangs in the Musée du Jeu de Paume in Paris and is one of Redon's most famous paintings.

Enclosed in this book you will find a large reproduction of this pastel. Use it as a pattern for this exercise.

Odilon Redon, (1840-1916) lithographer and painter, was born in Bordeaux and died in Paris. By about the year 1900 he had developed a style based on a mixture of reality and fantasy — a dreamlike quality. Some experts consider him to have been a precursor of surrealism — the imagery of the subconscious of which Salvador Dalí is the best known exponent. Redon, pupil of Gustave Moreau and Fantin-Latour, practised the techniques of etching and lithography. From 1900 onwards, he used his love of botany (stemming from studies of the botanist Clevand) and became a master in flower painting. His new system of gloriously rich colouring has been imitated by later famous artists.

Redon was a true dreamer of dreams and seer of visions. Germain Bazin, writer and curator of the Louvre, explains that Redon's flower groupings always contained a mixture of reality and fantasy. The reality comes from the artist's vision of his subject; the fantasy comes from what he wishes to see. With this in mind, it doesn't seem strange that Redon should see more colour than there really was. And one can understand why he painted yellow poppies although they weren't in the vase — and scattered all those little white flowers over his background. He wrote: "My flowers are born from the meeting of reality and memory. This merging is the land of art, the good land, cultivated by the spirit".

Reality and fantasy

This work was painted when Redon's style had reached maturity. We know that he died poor and forgotten, but should we really believe he could not afford something as essential as drawing paper? If you go to Paris and look at the original painting, hanging in the Impressionist section of the Louvre, you may be staggered to notice that this lovely flower painting was made on wrapping paper! The upper, lighter-coloured background is the colour of the paper itself — you can see the coarse grain of cheap wrapping paper. And today, that painting is worth about £30,000.

A picture of great value, painted on wrapping paper

Let us start the exercise — the copying of this pastel. We'll use our usual squaring up method to get a postcard-size reproduction of the print, following the example of the professional. So:

It is important to measure the squares exactly, because precision of that pattern depends upon it

1. Square up the enclosed print.
2. Enlarge your squared copy to the right size. Draw this on thin white paper and back it with sienna pastel or sanguine.
3. Trace the drawing onto the final drawing paper; use a charcoal pencil to complete it.
4. Paint your picture with pastels.

Some explanation is needed here. Why the tracing paper stage? The answer is simple — working this way you can avoid blurred corrections on your final paper.

The final drawing paper should, ideally, be as follows:

Pink or yellow-ochre Ingres Paper, mounted on thick cardboard measuring: 341 × 485 mm.

This is the minimum requirement. It is, however, possible to work on non-mounted paper — the final result will be almost the same.

Let's move on to the first step, but just let me explain the two ideas mentioned in sections 2 and 3.

WHY DO YOU DRAW, IN THE FIRST PLACE, ON THIN WHITE PAPER?

You may well ask, why do I have to draw the picture on thin white paper, instead of drawing it direct on the final paper? It's simply so that you can avoid corrections, blurring, rough rubbings and going over work again with the pencil, etc., on the final paper, and so ensure that the latter remains in its perfect state and thus provides a better result for the pastel colours.

WHAT DO WE UNDERSTAND BY "FINAL DRAWING PAPER"?

What kind, colour and thickness should it be? Has it to be fastened to a thick piece of cardboard which supplies stiffness and resistance?

The final drawing paper should be as follows:

Ingres paper, pink or ochre, if possible mounted on thick cardboard measuring exactly 341 × 485 millimetres.

It is perfectly all right for you to work on paper which isn't mounted on cardboard and you can be sure that the result will be almost the same.

SQUARED UP POSTCARD-SIZE COPY OF THE REDON PASTEL

YOU WILL NEED: a 2B pencil; a ruler and a set-square.

Measurement: 7 × 10 squares (1.5 cm each)

Cut out the postcard size reproduction (p. 19) of Redon's painting. Square this up, allowing 1.5 cm to each square. You should then have a pattern of 7 × 10 squares.

Be accurate

Try to draw these squares with perfect accuracy. A millimetre here and there *does* count —your flowers will not be right unless you have measured exactly. Think of this job as part of your apprenticeship.

This is the professional way to square up your picture:

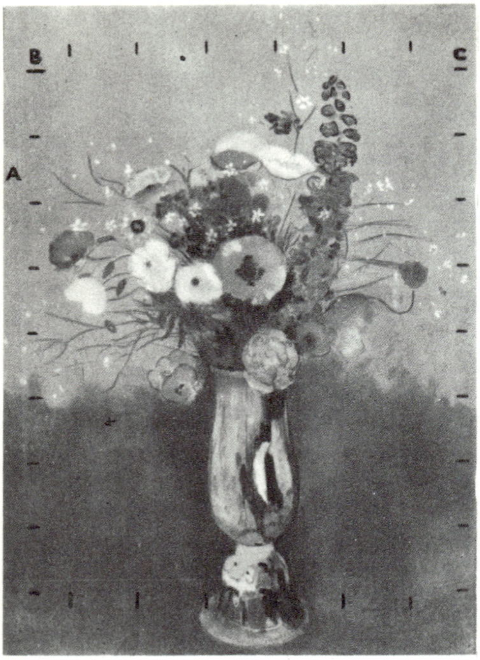

I. With the help of the graduated ruler mark off the sections with strongly-marked small strokes up and down and on the right and left-hand sides of the picture (see illustration left).

II. Draw the horizontal lines with the ruler and set-square, placing the ruler down vertically first of all and lining it up with margin A and then placing the set-square up against the ruler, forming a right-angle, to check that the lines B and C are perfectly placed in relation to the edge of the set-square. Then draw in the top line, and slide the triangle downwards to draw in the subsequent lines.

III. Then draw in the vertical lines, using the same system.

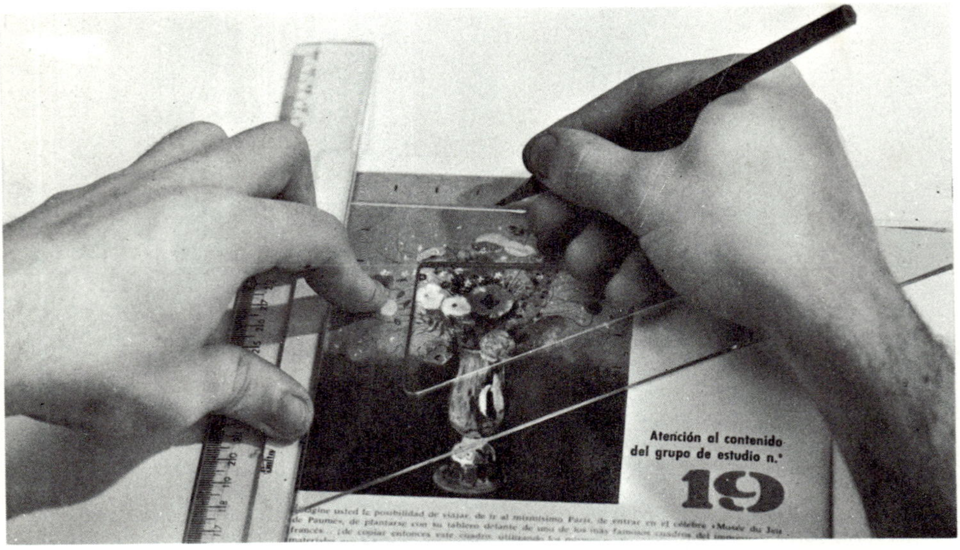

So that the measurements can be reproduced exactly, the subject is divided up into squares by placing the set square up against the ruler, (illustration above).

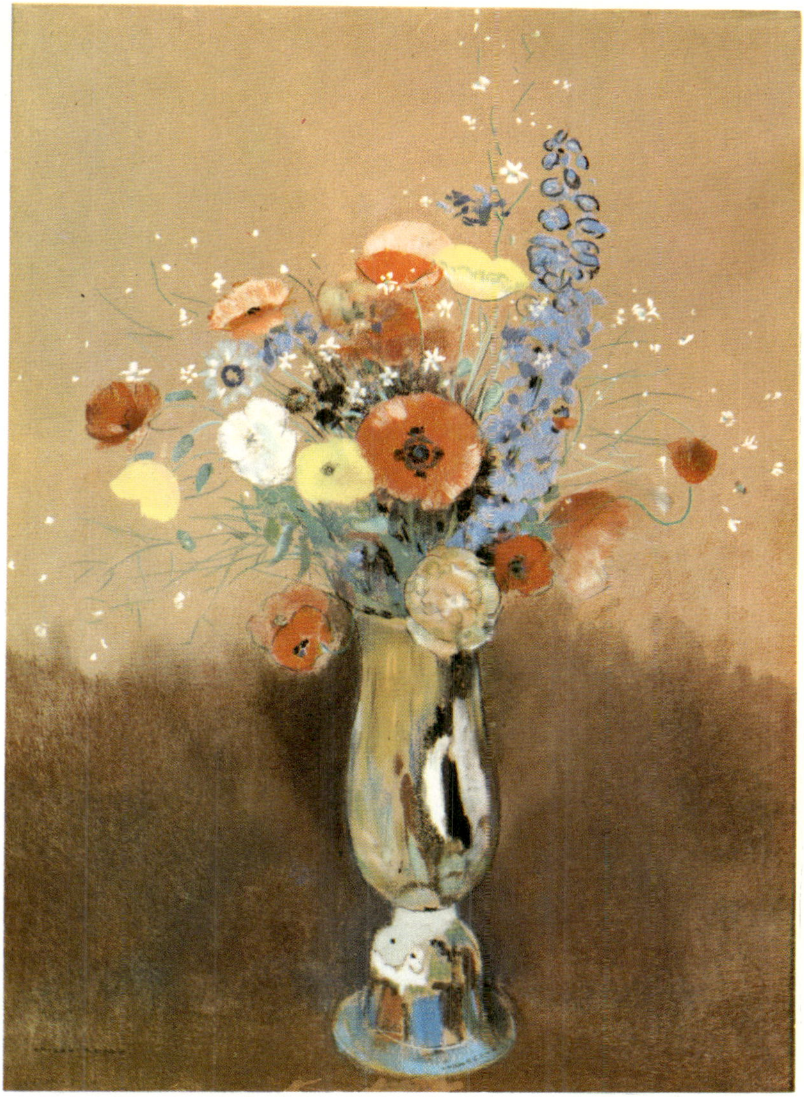

CUT ALONG DOTTED LINES

Remove page from book. Take out picture by cutting along dotted lines.

Then square up this postcard-size print into squares as shown in a and b opposite This is the professional method of copying a picture, in this case, Redon's flower pastel.

SQUARING UP AND ENLARGING USING TRACING PAPER

First decide your final measurements say: 48 × 33.5 cm

The tracing paper and final paper need to be larger than your measured picture, otherwise you will tend to paint over the edges. The margin can be cut off afterwards:

For example:

Enlarged squaring up system: 7 × 10 sq; 4,8 cm each

if your picture is to be 48 × 33.5 cm, tracing and drawing paper should measure 48.5 × 34.1 cm.

Or you may wish the tracing and final drawing paper to be larger by about 3 cm for edging and fitting the tracing paper against the final drawing paper.

This may be cleared up if you look at p. 24 which shows your squaring-up diagram.

Now, draw a rectangle 48 × 33.5 cm on tracing paper. Divided in proportions of 10 and 7 (10 sq high × 7 sq wide) this will give you a system of 4.8 cm squares. Check your measurements.

Squaring up on tracing paper is done like this:

Enlarge using squares

1. Mark out sections 4.8 cm on a piece of paper to form a sort of graduated ruler.

2. Using this, transfer the sections to the tracing paper; you should have seven sections across and ten down.

Once you've got your accurate squares, go ahead with your soft pencil, using the squares to enlarge each section of the picture. Then colour the back of the tracing paper with sienna pastel or sanguine sticks, covering and shading with your fingers until the reverse is covered and will leave its mark like carbon paper.

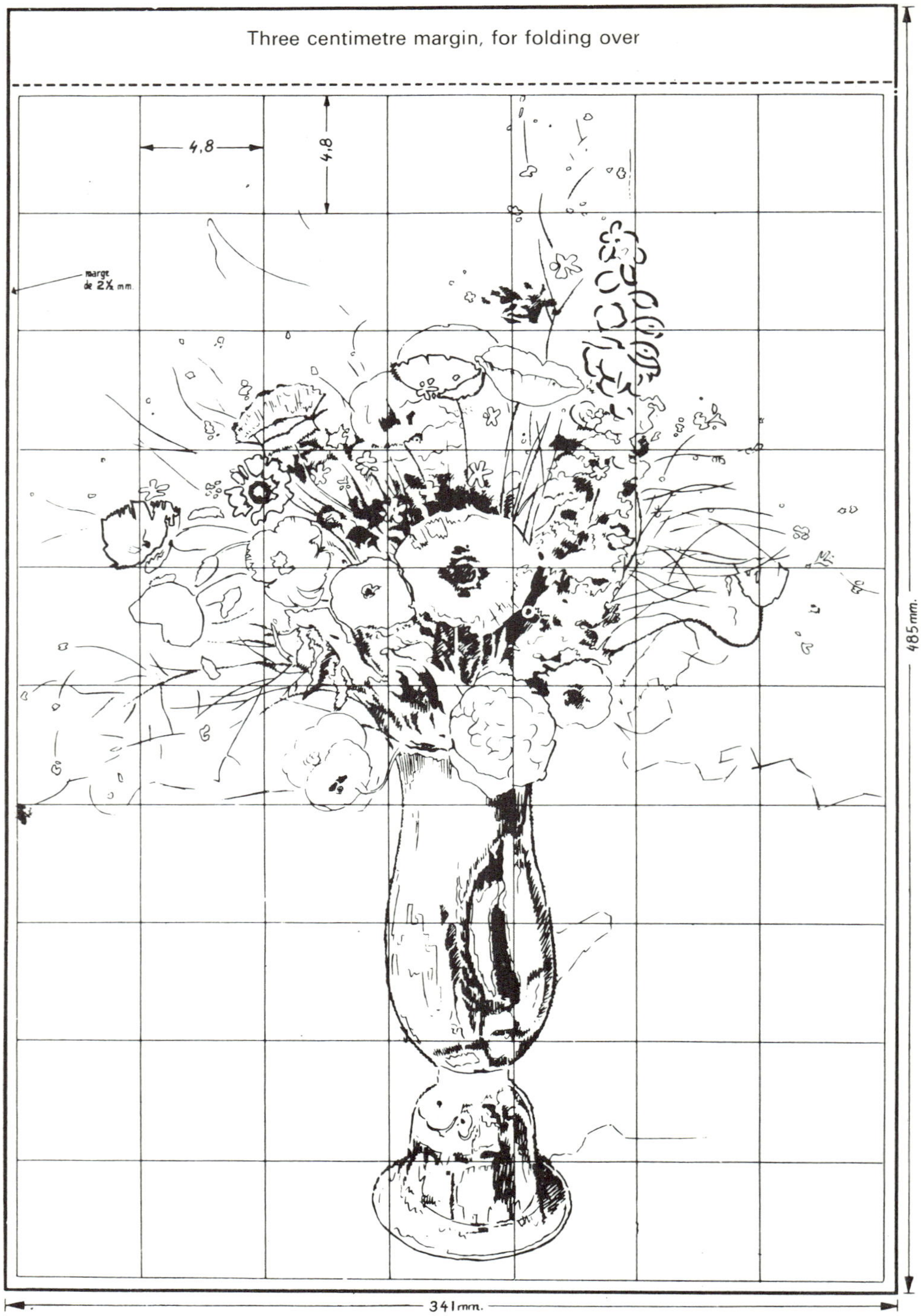

AN EXAMPLE OF ENLARGING WITH SQUARED PAPER

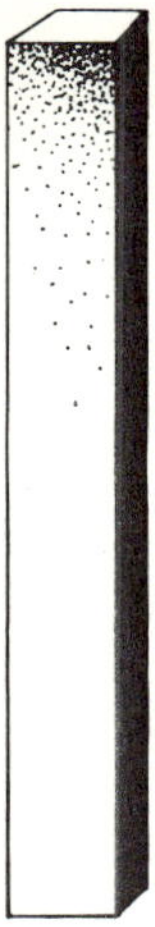

I should have mentioned that sanguine comes in square 6 mm sticks, about 7 cm long. It is very like pastel and, like charcoal, is used by itself for painting. If you have no sanguine, use a sienna or brown pastel — you'll get the same effect.

Place your home-made "carbon" paper over the final drawing paper, folding a 3 cm margin at the top. Secure this at the back. Then just trace your drawing with a soft pencil — obviously you don't trace the squares! Try not to use the heel of your hand too much, for the sanguine will smudge the drawing paper. Trace carefully to get a good result.

Final tracing onto drawing paper

FINAL STAGE: REPRODUCTION OF THE PAINTING

YOU WILL NEED: AN ORDINARY LEAD PENCIL; A CHARCOAL PENCIL; FIXATIVE AND FINAL DRAWING PAPER.

Prop the reproduction of Redon's pastel in front of you and try to imagine it's the real thing. Go over the outlines with the charcoal pencil. Look carefully at the colour print and try to make your own interpretation of each flower and leaf. Imagine the poppies and tiny blossoms are real. Then draw the bunch in greater detail, looking at the print and also at the close-up on p 26. You'll notice that the parts in shadow have been drawn in black and blended, using charcoal pencil — this should make it easier for you.

It is vital to try to interpret the form of every flower, leaf and stalk as strictly as you can.

Go over the construction again with a charcoal pencil

Try to reproduce the poppies, flowers and tiny blossoms which form the bunch as they really are. Then try to draw the bunch itself in greater detail, if possible, than that supplied by the picture itself. The previous figure will help here. Also consult the coloured reproduction on page 29, which corresponds to the first stage.

You'll see that the dark, almost black, parts presented by the subject, have already been drawn in black, by the copying of shapes, blendings, etc., with the charcoal pencil. This is so that you may work with a more complete subject for reference.

Lastly, once everything has been well drawn, go ahead with your fixing with ordinary fixative for lead pencil and charcoal. The purpose of this fixing is to avoid later mixing of the lead pencil with the pastel colours. This can be achieved with very little liquid. Too much could damage the grain and finish of the paper.

Then you can get on with the painting.

POINTS TO REMEMBER

Difficulty and impossibility of workingh with the same quality of paper used by Redon

We might have wanted you to paint this picture on wrapping paper similar in type and quality to Redon's. But this seems inadvisable. It is difficult to find wrapping paper with a colour equal to that used in Redon's picture, and secondly because, even if the colour were similar, the quality (texture, grain, roughness, etc.) would not answer to the technique of pastel painting. We also thought that it wasn't suitable to base the apprenticeship to this technique on ordinary wrapping paper. Leave that to the expert.

Once the drawing is complete, use the fixative you would use for pencil and charcoal. This avoids later blending lead pencil with the pastel. Use as little fixative as possible.

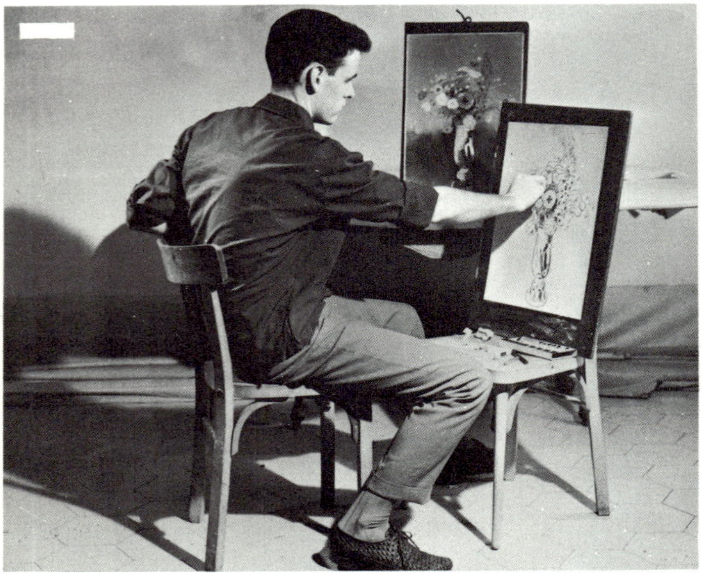

The illustration shows how to use a drawing board instead of an easel. Note the position of the painter's arm — out-stretched. He has placed his model beside him for easy reference.

STARTING TO PAINT

We are not using wrapping paper

Redon used wrapping paper for his painting. We are departing from his example — the right colour paper is hard to get hold of and the texture would be wrong. Also, following Redon's example would make things difficult for the beginner, although Redon or a professional would manage it with ease. The best substitute is the yellow-ochre Ingres paper. This makes a suitable background for all Redon's colours. Rose Ingres paper would be even better, but is very hard to find.

An easel is not vital for your work

You may not have an easel. The illustration opposite shows how to make do with two ordinary chairs and a drawing board. Fix the final paper to the drawing board with drawing pins. Use the front of the chair to hold your box of pastels, charcoal pencil and your clean rag for erasing. You'll need to have your model picture standing vertically to your left, or hanging on the wall beside you.

PRACTISE BEFORE YOU START

It's a good idea to try out your pastels on a bit of rough paper before you begin the final painting. Get used to the method of portraying light and shade, shading with your fingers and trying out some line drawing too. Try to match your colours with those of the model; analyse how the blue patches are a mixture of different blues. Find the best yellow for the poppies, the best green for the leaves.

Once you are ready to start, position the print enclosed in this book so that you can easily copy it, as in the illustration opposite.

Reproduction of Odile Redon's painting Wild flowers in a long necked vase.

Do your best to copy the painting. Put it by you near where you are working.

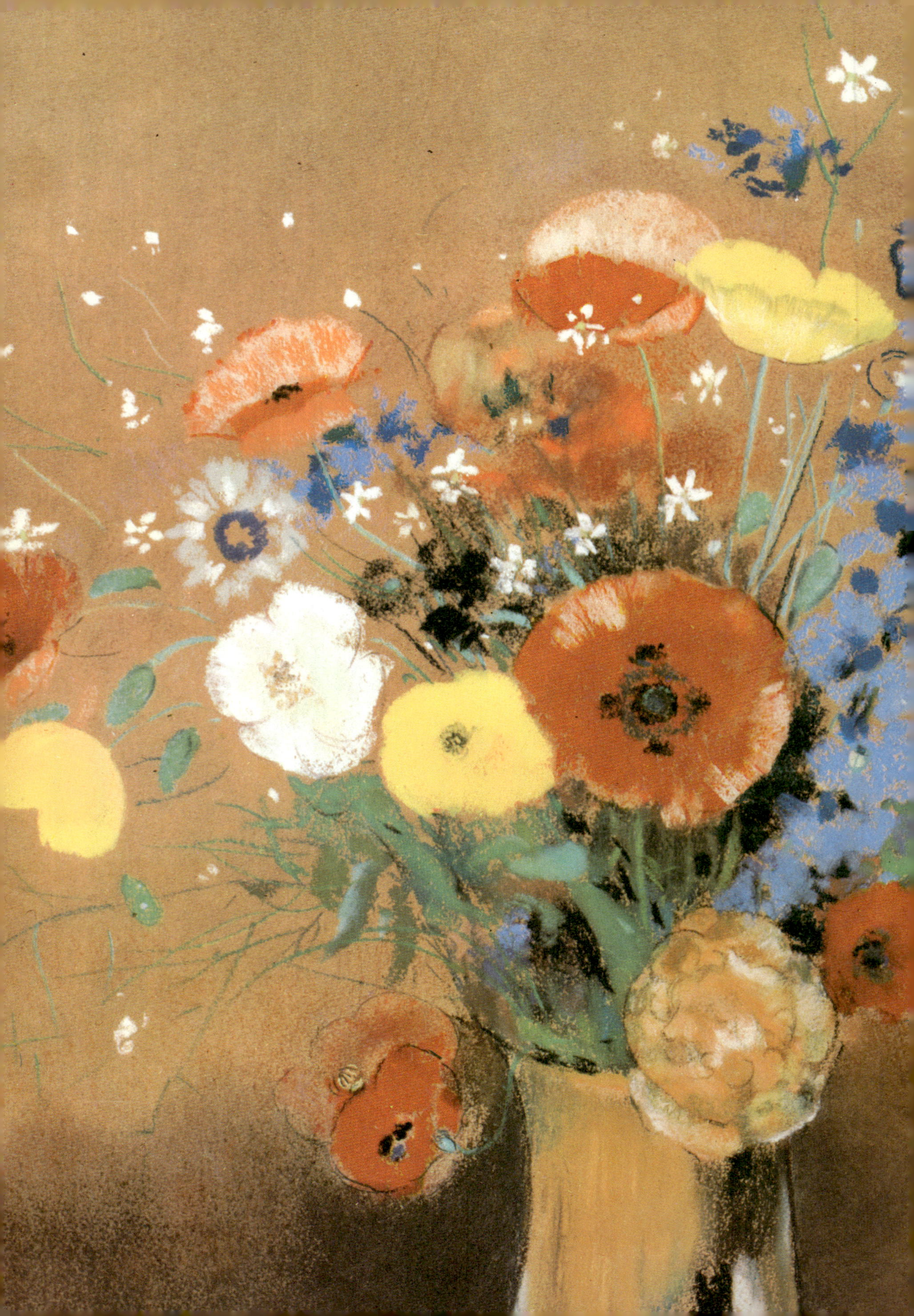

STAGE 1. CHECK YOUR COLOURS AGAINST THOSE OF THE PICTURE.

You'll find you'll need them all, as well as the charcoal pencil.

Colours and method of working

Basic: red ochre.

UPPER BACKGROUND

This kind of deep flesh colour is supplied in all pastel boxes. Use it for the upper background, rubbing the surface with a flat piece and shading off with your fingers — like a wash for a watercolour. Use a thin layer to start with, thickening it later.

You'll need a little white, as well,
because red ochre alone provides a rather dark and gloomy background. Mix a little white with the ochre, then shade off very gently; this will give you the right background colour.

Don't worry about going over the edges

Don't worry about taking your background colour over the edges of leaves, etc. Just try to leave some wide spaces for the large flowers. You'll be able to paint over the background with both lighter and darker colours.

Light yellow

You can mix this in with the background colours; it gives a brighter effect.

LOWER BACKGROUND

Orange and light vermilion

This helps your background, too. Use orange very lightly in the sections near the cluster of flowers. Use the light vermilion in the parts near the darker shading and for the shadow behind the vase.

Sanguine, vermilion, carmine, orange, Prussian blue, dark green and black.

If you look carefully at the lower, darker part of the background in your print, you'll notice it has two basic colours —

VASE

sanguine (or dark sienna) and black. Under these, there's a hint of Prussian blue and dark green, and, on the left of the vase, you can make out a mixture of orange and yellow. There's also a hint of shaded vermilion and carmine in the background, especially at the top, where the light and shade meet.

Red ochre

Keep your line drawing

Paint the vase with red ochre using this very lightly in the bits overlaid with other colours. Don't worry about going over the edges. You can apply white, blue, black and so on afterwards. But when you paint the background over the part which will have outlines, try to preserve the pattern you made with your charcoal pencil. Go over the lines very lightly with charcoal pencil so that your pattern doesn't get completely lost.

The picture shown opposite is in its first colour stage — I've left it after blending the background and painting the vase with red ochre, so that you can see the different stages. Then, look overleaf at the picture in its second and more advanced stage. You'll note that the blending is finished, contrasts appear and colours have been intensified. This is how it was done.

Vermilion, light vermilion and white

RED POPPIES

Use vermilion as a base, mix light vermilion, mixed with white or alone, for the light parts.

...and carmine

in small quantities to intensify the red of the red parts.

Light yellow, chrome yellow and white

YELLOW POPPIES

Light yellow is your basic colour. Try to paint and shape at the same time and don't worry about any lack of uniformity.

Black pastel and charcoal pencil

DARK CENTRES

Contrasts are needed for the bits in the centre of the flowers; also, the part round the centre red poppy needs black shading. First sketch over in black pastel, pressing fairly hard and then intensify these parts by going over them in charcoal pencil.

Wash the tip of your fingers

N.B. You'll need to wash your hands from time to time, or your fingers will tinge light colours with dark.

Fig.7

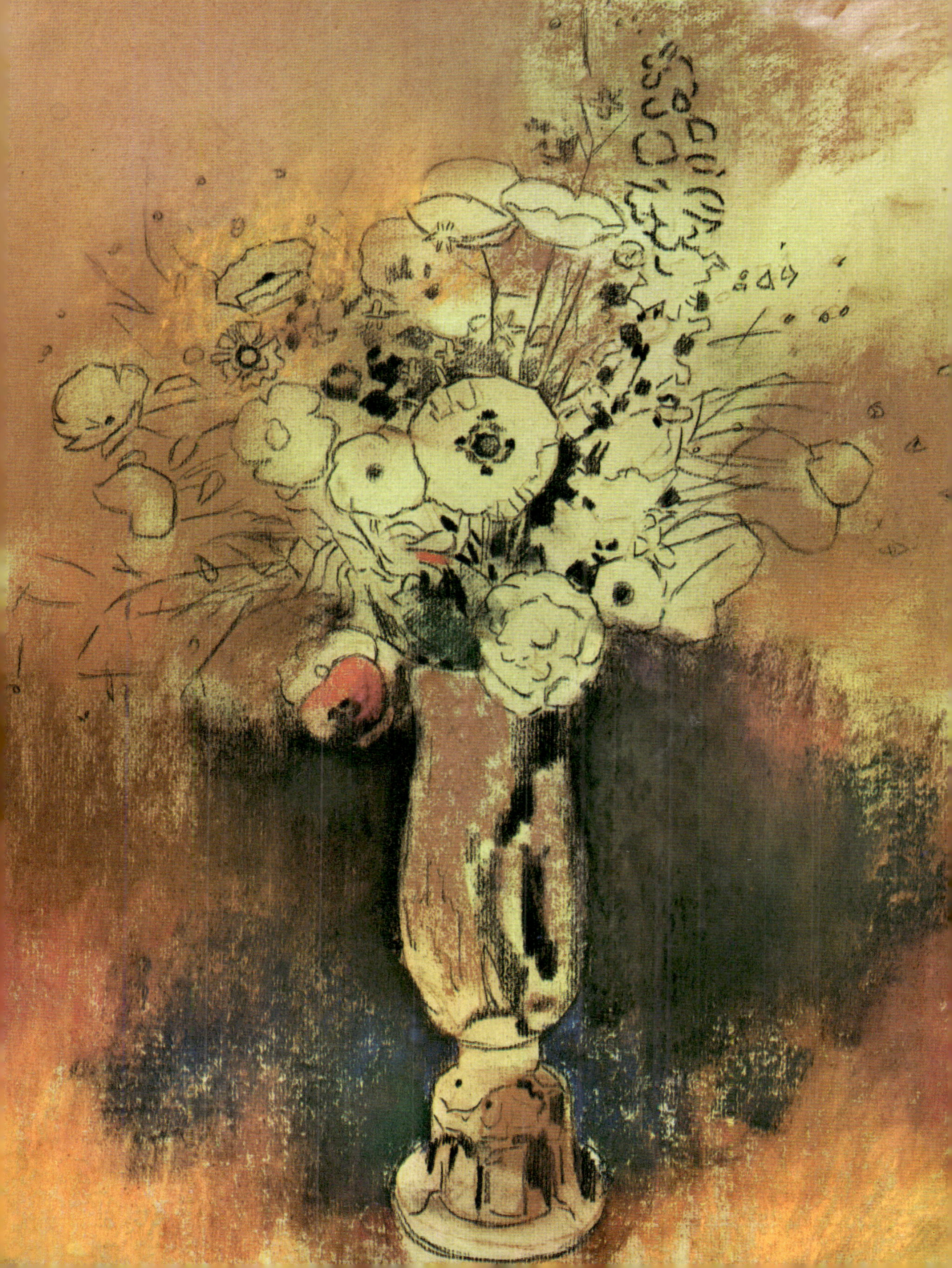

Clean the points of your pastels to avoid blurring colours

You'll need to clean the tips of the pastel colours with a rag. Otherwise you'll find you're painting with light yellow instead of chrome yellow. If the pastel edges get dirty it's only too easy to make this mistake.

GREEN LEAVES

First of all, use *dark green*

Use this to paint the leaf shapes very faintly. Using fingers, blur dark green with the dark part under the central poppy.

Then use *light green*

To highlight parts of the leaves.

Finally, use *sky blue*

This should be mixed with light green to intensify the brightness of some leaves. Don't shade this off; use broad covering pastel strokes.

White

WHITE FLOWER

For the time being, don't use your pure white pastel — keep the centre part of the flower untouched until later, but use your stick for shaping the outline.

Sky blue:

TALL BLUE FLOWER

Start by carefully brush-shaping the cluster of blue flowers. Try not to shade off, but to try to make a faithful copy of Redon's strokes and shaping in this section. Remember that you are copying, so don't fly off at a tangent, however tempting!

Ultramine:

Use this to cover most of your sky-blue flower — mix it slightly to darken the bloom.

Charcoal pencil:

Look carefully at Redon's thick dark lines. Try to get absolute accuracy in placing and intensity.

Prussian blue and ultramarine:

Use this mixture to paint in the darker blue patches, especially the flowers nestling round the bottom of the stalk.

Umber:

This is a greyish chestnut which you should use for intensifying some of the dark-blue sections.

Red ochre, light vermilion, yellow and orange:

You'll need these shades for the paler part of the vase neck. Keeping yellow as your base, mix a little light vermilion and orange; here you can use a little white, which should help produce that deep

REF. 8

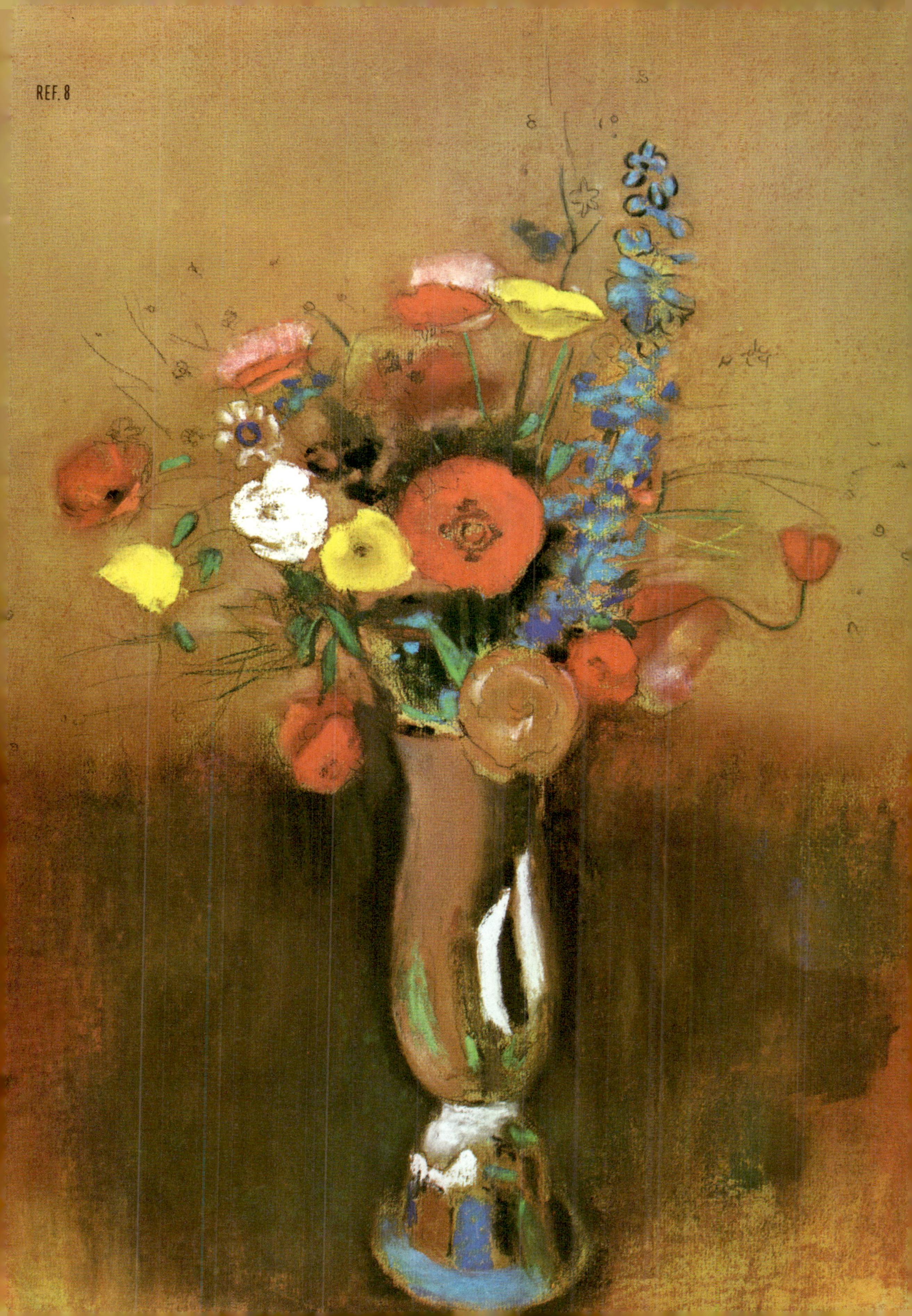

flesh colour. Study the print carefully and use these colours for the darker side with the white reflexions and the black and sienna patches.

NECK OF THE VASE

Charcoal:

Once you've blended the pastels on the lighter side, use charcoal for the black shadows and the grey-black shading on the right-hand side of the neck.

Sanguine and black pastel:

Go on colouring those long brown patches. You'll see in the print that the various colours painted over the red ochre background are hardly toned down. You can allow yourself a little boldness here.

Light green:

Press fairly hard with this. Mix it, without toning down, into the background — you'll see it almost disappears.

White and burnt umber:

When colouring the vase, use white as in the two patches in the print; use burnt umber in the more shaded area, together with white, sanguine and black.

Remove dust

Remember to stop work from time to time in order to remove the fine dust, using light taps with the cardboard against the ground, or some hard object. You can do a certain amount of this by just blowing into the coloured parts. Remember also the way to erase — using a soft, clean piece of cotton.

BACKGROUND DARKER PART

Sanguine and black:

Keep returning to this darker background. It's useful for creating contrasts because you can deepen it where it borders on the lighter vase.

PINK FLOWER

Red ochre, light vermilion, pink, light yellow and white:

We're talking about the slightly fuzzy pink flower just below the centre poppy. You'll need to mix these colours, drawing in the flower's shape and reinforcing the fine dark lines with charcoal.

BASE OF VASE

Red ochre:

Apply a fine layer but be careful not to erase the initial drawing.

Sanguine, natural umber and black:

Check the model carefully and use these colours as needed, remembering the sienna and the greyish tones. Each patch of colour has its own shade, so study the picture carefully. You'll see that almost all the colour patches at the base of the vase were painted without toning down (except for the white).

Light and dark green:

If you look carefully, you'll be able to pick out these greens on the upper part of the base. To dampen the bright colour down a bit, you can mix in a little sanguine.

Prussian blue

This is straightforward: paint in the rectangular patch.

Sky blue and Prussian blue

You'll notice these colours on the base of the vase. First, apply soft layer of Prussian blue and then use the sky blue, pressing quite hard.

STAGE 2: USE THE SHAPE OF YOUR SUBJECT TO HELP CREATE VOLUME AND CONTRASTS

This can make the colours more intense.

THE BASICS **ARE THE SAME AS BEFORE.**

Contrasts

You'll be able to finish off the picture yourself, working as before. Just go on adding colours and painting in sections with the print as your model. It's quite an easy model, without colour mixing. But there are one or two bits of advice you may find useful:

Paint slender stems in greens or yellows

You may find that a colour doesn't stand out enough to be interesting. That may well be due to lack of contrast in your painting. The subject should stand out of the background, as it were. You just add a bit of colour, using more pastel and exaggerating the chiaroscuro. Any black should be painted in absolute black.

Keep the slender stalks and little white flowers until you have nearly finished — add them as a finishing touch. The little stems can be painted dark or light green, or, if you like, in chrome or very light and bright yellow. Check your pastel stick for a good edge and make sure you have a steady hand! You might find it easier at this stage to leave your substitute easel and work on a flat surface. Paint the little flowers petal by petal, copying accurately.

Pastel can be covered

Sometimes you'll find that a certain colour, a red flower, for example, impinges on the background. Just paint over it with red ochre, thickening the outlines, or daub it hard on the section to be covered.

More haste, less speed

Remember the phrase 'more haste, less speed'. It's not a good idea to paint in a single sitting. Paint the first stage, leave a day and then, with a fresh mind, go on and finish the painting, touching up as needed.

When you've done all that, your painting will be finished, for there can be no fixing process with pastel. Take a critical look at your work — it's always a sound idea. You may well find things to change a little. How's it gone? An enjoyable task anyway.

WAX COLOURS:

BASIC INFORMATION

Pigments and wax fused together by heat

Wax colours are made of pigments and colouring substances moulded and held together by wax and other greasy substances. This mixing takes place at fixed heat and forms a paste which dries out into neat sticks of colour. It's not so unlike the colours with which the primitive cave artist decorated his walls at Altamira, in the north of Spain, where the most marvellous paintings of animals were discovered at the end of the last century.

Several paint manufacturers also make wax colours, and there are some who specialize in this medium, among them Caran d'Ache and Faber. The basic difference between the various brands is one of durability. This, in turn, affects technique in several ways.

Permanency and covering properties

Most wax colours are more or less permanent — colouring with them is by rubbing and they have good covering properties. You can apply a light colour over a dark one and get a slight merging of colour. This covering quality is found more in the softer brands, reminding one of pastel.

How to buy wax colours

Wax colours are made in cylindrical sticks of different sizes. The usual thickness is like an ordinary pencil, or slightly thicker, with the length varying between five and twelve cms. They come in boxes of assorted colours containing six, twelve, eighteen, twenty-four and thirty-six colours. The normal assortment for the amateur is a box of twelve colours, including black and white.

Potential

Because of their covering properties and their permanency, wax colours have great potential; they are most often used for colouring small pictures. They are an ideal medium for rough sketches which are going to be enlarged — noted for later use in large projects, murals, for instance. They are also used for scaled-down murals which will eventually be painted in oils. They are marvellous for 'catching' a colour and their richness reminds one of oil paintings. They are used for portraits — finishing off the head and sketching in the body — and are also useful for book illustrations and commercial art.

They are also a useful medium to use with Indian ink. Wax crayons can be used on paper, canvas, wood, etc.; but the most usual use is on white or tinted paper. The paper must be hard and slightly rough-grained so that the pigments and wax will adhere easily.

Paper is the best surface

These colours cannot be removed with india-rubber; correcting small areas can be done with a knife or razor blade — we'll go into that later.

The colours can be fixed with a special plastic varnish used with a brush. This gives the picture a slightly shining patina like a varnished oil painting. But fixing is not essential, as wax colours are practically permanent. One more point — it's obvious but might not occur to one — the wax colours and paintings must be protected from prolonged heat and from bright sunlight.

Fixing

Avoid heat

HOW TO START

Different brands have different degrees of hardness and this means that a slightly different technique must be used with different brands of colours. It's rather like using coloured pencils — the same mixture of colours happens when you paint one colour over another. This mixing is easier with wax crayons because they give a softer quality to the painting. You can use fingers for toning and

Similarity of technique between wax colours and pastel

graduating light and shade. This can't really be done with coloured pencils.

The technique of painting with wax colours has great links with that for pastels, particularly when soft wax is used. Colours can be mixed like liquid paints. The application of white over any colour diminishes its intensity and produces a grey tone. Also, fingers can be used in the same way and the wax can make a dense covering. The stability of wax colours should be kept in mind — they can't be erased easily like pastels. They are quite different in results, though the technique is similar.

BASIC TECHNIQUE — A SUMMARY

Start by painting bold lines without shading. These strokes are painted over the basic melange of colours and the shading will come when you are using cyan blue for the dark areas.

Mix with your fingers

Then alternate your firm strokes with finger mixing — you'll need to paint fairly thickly so that there is enough colour to come off on your fingers.

Use white for basic harmony

White is the useful harmonizing shade and it's easy to make into a paste. Beware though — white is so malleable that things can get grey almost while your back is turned!

Use a razor blade for erasing

Erasing cannot be done with rubbers —you have to scrape colour off with a knife or razor blade. It won't all come off, but you can paint over the faint remains of the colour.

Keep your colours clean

With certain colours — for example, yellow, you have to be specially careful about mixing, because the wax may get heaped up and the area will lack uniformity. These patches of wax can be removed with a clean rag.

Keep everything clean

Soft wax crayons get softer from the heat of the hand. The natural way to paint is to hold a few colours in your left hand while painting with the right. But this means that white and other pale colours can get rubbed off on each other. A pale stick of wax will itself get tinged when working over a darker colour — you have to clean it with a rag. Since you are using your fingers as artist's tools, you have to clean them from time to time, especially when shading with a pale colour.

Clothes must be sensible or you won't be comfortable. Wear an artist's smock or some old clothes — grease from the colours sticks to fabric and is difficult to get rid of.

Wear working clothes

There's one trick of the trade you might find useful. We've said that colour may be removed by a knife or blade. If you want initial highlights — clear outlined highlights — painted in white, and you find that colour goes over the edges of your highlight, simply remove the colour with a razor blade. Then you'll see your white patch safe and sound. You can use this method for smaller details too — a light-coloured mast, white caps on waves lapping at the shore, tiny flowers. This trick can be taken further, for faces, animals, plants, etc. Use very light green and cover with a darker green. Then simply scrape your white outlines with your blade.

Usefulness of colour can show through — scraping is useful

It's possible to combine wax colouring with Indian ink — draw in ink and then paint. Combined with petrol you can overlap diluted films of wax on the same sheet, providing great delicacy and transparency of colour.

Combine with Indian ink or dilute with turps

The best way of putting all this into practice is to try for yourself on rough, grained paper approximately 25 × 35 cm. Or you can use larger surfaces when dealing with wax paints and that mixture of drawing and painting needed for publication.

FROM THEORY TO PRACTICE

WAX PAINTING OF A STILL LIFE ARRANGED BY THE READER.

YOU WILL NEED: DRAWING PAPER; HB PENCIL; ROUGH PAPER FOR FIRST SKETCHES; BOX OF 12 WAX COLOURS; A RAZOR BLADE.

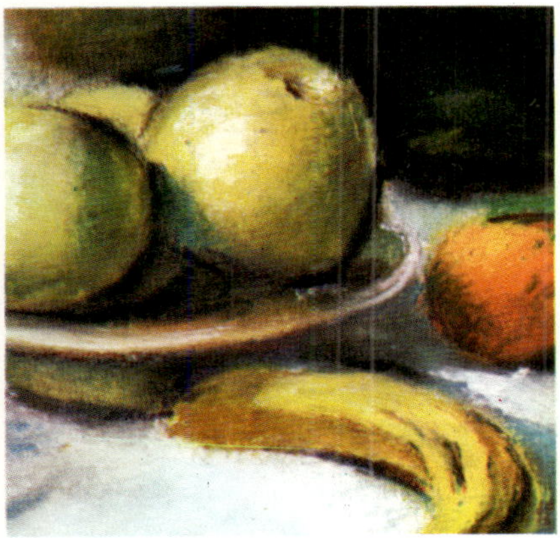

Check back to the technique mentioned for pastel painting. This is similar to the technique for wax colouring. Remember that pastel is ephemeral compared with wax. The two techniques separate when it comes to mixing, shading and superimposing one colour on another. The differences are interesting.

On the next page is shown the range of colours usually found in an assortment of twelve:

white
medium cadmium yellow
orange
red
carmine
violet
cyan blue
ultramarine
green
yellow ochre
burnt sienna
black

Let's try out this medium with a few exercises using drawing paper or rough grainy paper.

I. Using cyan blue, paint a patch of colour like the patch A, facing page.

II. Soften this patch with your fingers, fairly hard, to get a regular tone (B). You'll see that the pressure of the fingers makes the colour sticky and almost melted.

III. Now paint white over the blue patch. This demonstrates the method of painting with a light colour over a dark one (C).

IV. Rub the white with your fingers and see how clear the colour is (D).

V. Now use carmine, yellow, ochre, etc. on top of the cyan blue patch, using your fingers and experimenting with covering and mixing one colour with others (E).

VI. Lastly, use a penknife or razor blade on these last patches of colour. Compare the first blue and the last blue (F).

In a final experiment you can draw and paint using a razor blade for your pen.

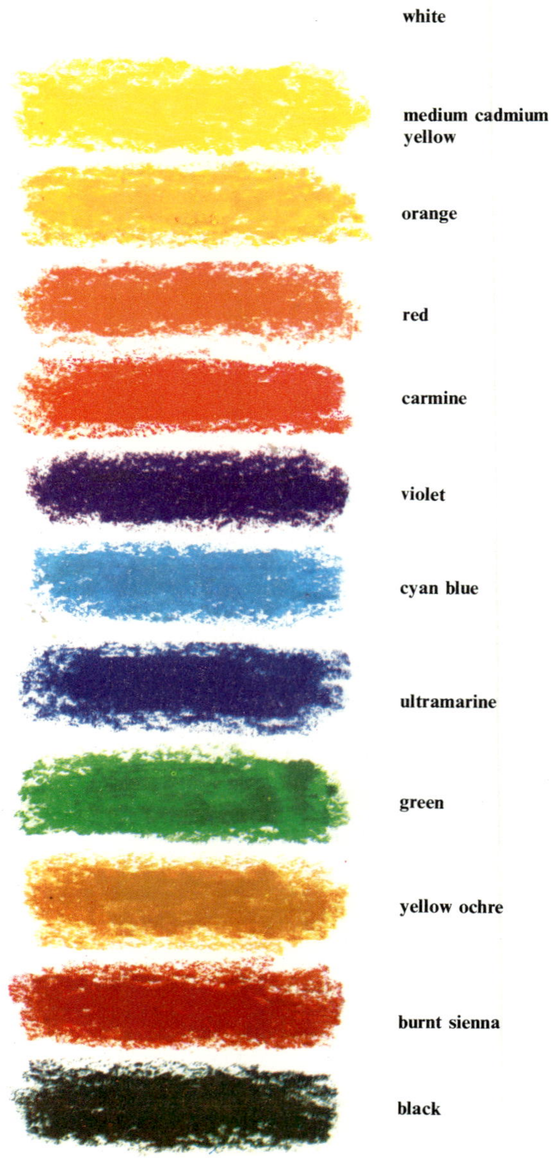

You can also get pure white by painting the white patch first, then superimposing other colours and finally scraping them off with a razor blade.

So we can now go ahead with the first picture painted with wax colours.

Use cartridge paper, or good quality card with a slightly rough finish.

FIG. 2

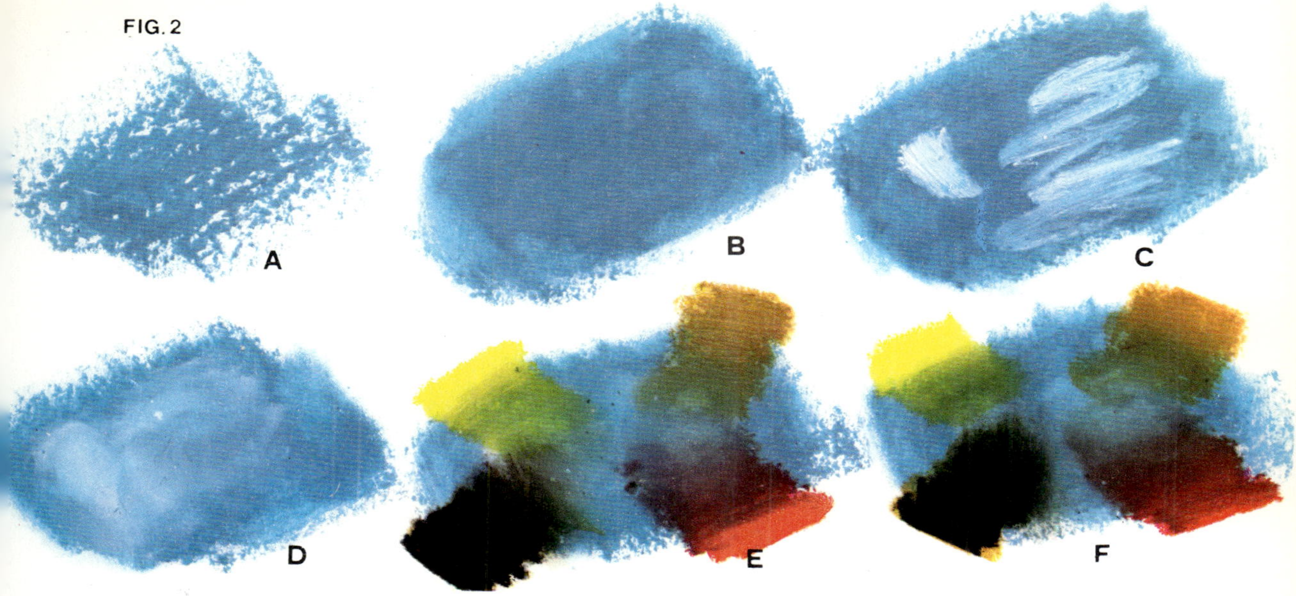

FROM THEORY TO PRACTICE

Study your subject and then draw and paint a sketch.

First of all, go ahead with choosing the model and studying its composition. Draw a few rough sketches, choose the best of them and then paint it using wax colours. Work, for the time being, on a reduced scale on cartridge type paper or similar. Use small sketches measuring approximately 10 × 15 cm.

Study composition and harmonizing in a sketch 10 × 15 cm

When I painted the still life shown on pp. 46, 47, and 48, I began by studying the model and composition using small colour marks painted in wax. You can see these marks in the figures overleaf, reproduced in black and white. You'll notice that I first tried to use a glass carafe, a pestle and mortar and a few pimentos for my model. Then I increased the number of components — adding some and taking away others. This last sketch decided me upon the final composition; I added an earthenware bowl and removed an orange, slightly altering the position of the carafe with the apples and other components of my still life.

SECOND STAGE: USING ALL THE WAX COLOURS

It's a good idea to begin painting with just the cyan blue crayon, using it to paint all the parts in shadow or the dark areas of the model. This helps break up the pure white of your paper and also fulfils the rule that blue should be present in all shading.

Use cyan blue to start with

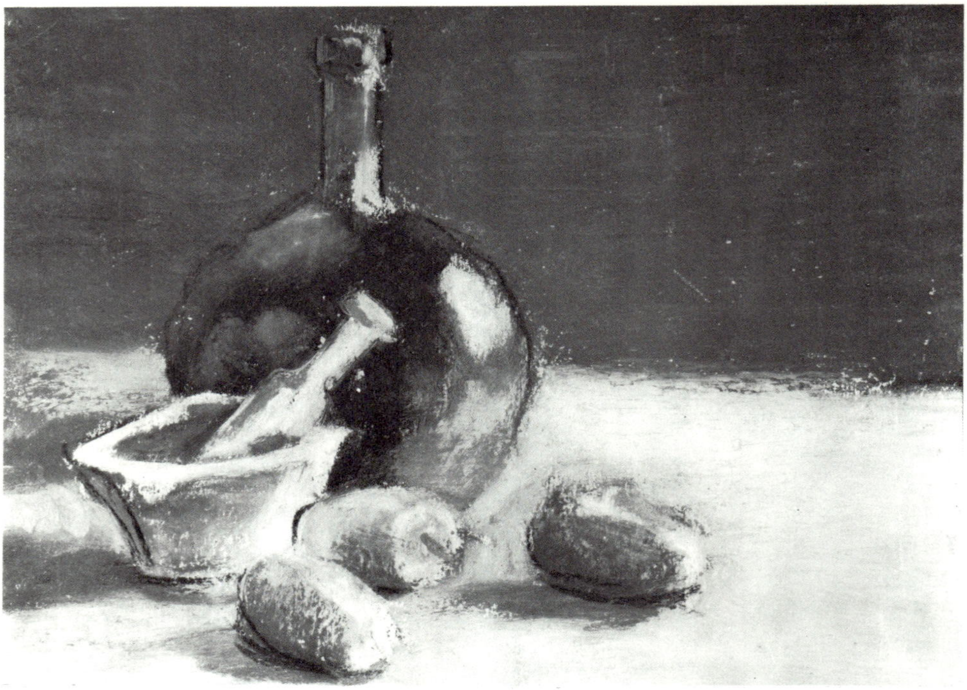

3

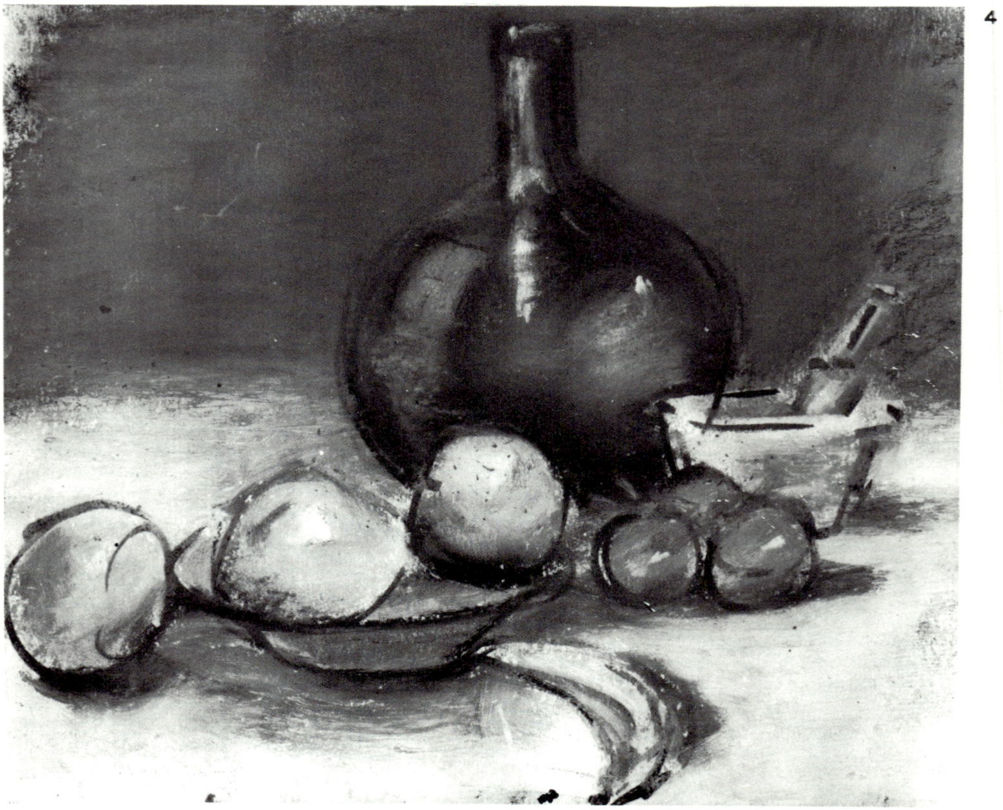

4

Then paint over this first layer of cyan blue, using the colours you need at each stage.
I. - Draw direct, without shading off yet.
II. - Don't worry about going over the edges.
III. - For the moment keep it simple, and move on from small things to larger.

THIRD STAGE: GENERAL INTENSIFICATION OF COLOUR

Now use more vigorous strokes and accumulate a larger amount of material (wax and grease) so that you can make a paste of it with your fingers, also using them to shade your sketch. To make composite colours like khaki, bluish grey, greyish green, etc., begin by tracing with one colour and then tone down. Trace again with the same colour or with another and tone down again with your fingers. Then, when the colour becomes greasy to the touch, it's easy to add a little blue, yellow, red or ochre or whatever you need to compose the colouring.

Now draw more vigorously and accumulate more material

Try to shape with your fingers as though they were brushes. This will often involve going over the edge of other colours. This doesn't matter. In its warm state, when the medium is semi-liquid, it is easy to correct, sketch outlines and draw with your fingers. You can help out from time to time with a direct touch from a stick of crayon. You are more likely to succeed with a sketch in which there is some feeling, with under-stressed outlines, than have a cold sketch that is just outline.

Shade off with your fingers

You should paint the picture all in one go, trying to work from start to finish. Don't stop or postpone painting any section until you have finished it.

FOURTH AND LAST STAGE: ADJUSTMENT AND FINISHING

Allow twenty-four hours or as long as you can between stage three and this one. Adjust the colouring and try to see all the possible shades.

Enrich the colouring

Carefully observe the colours reflected in the shadows. Try to make outlines stand out by using contrasts.

Now create a sense of atmosphere by thinning the outlines of the most distant elements, which is easy to do if you work with your fingers, and by emphasizing the outline of the nearest elements.

Contrast and atmosphere

I made some notes while I was painting a still life with wax and it might be useful to go through them here.

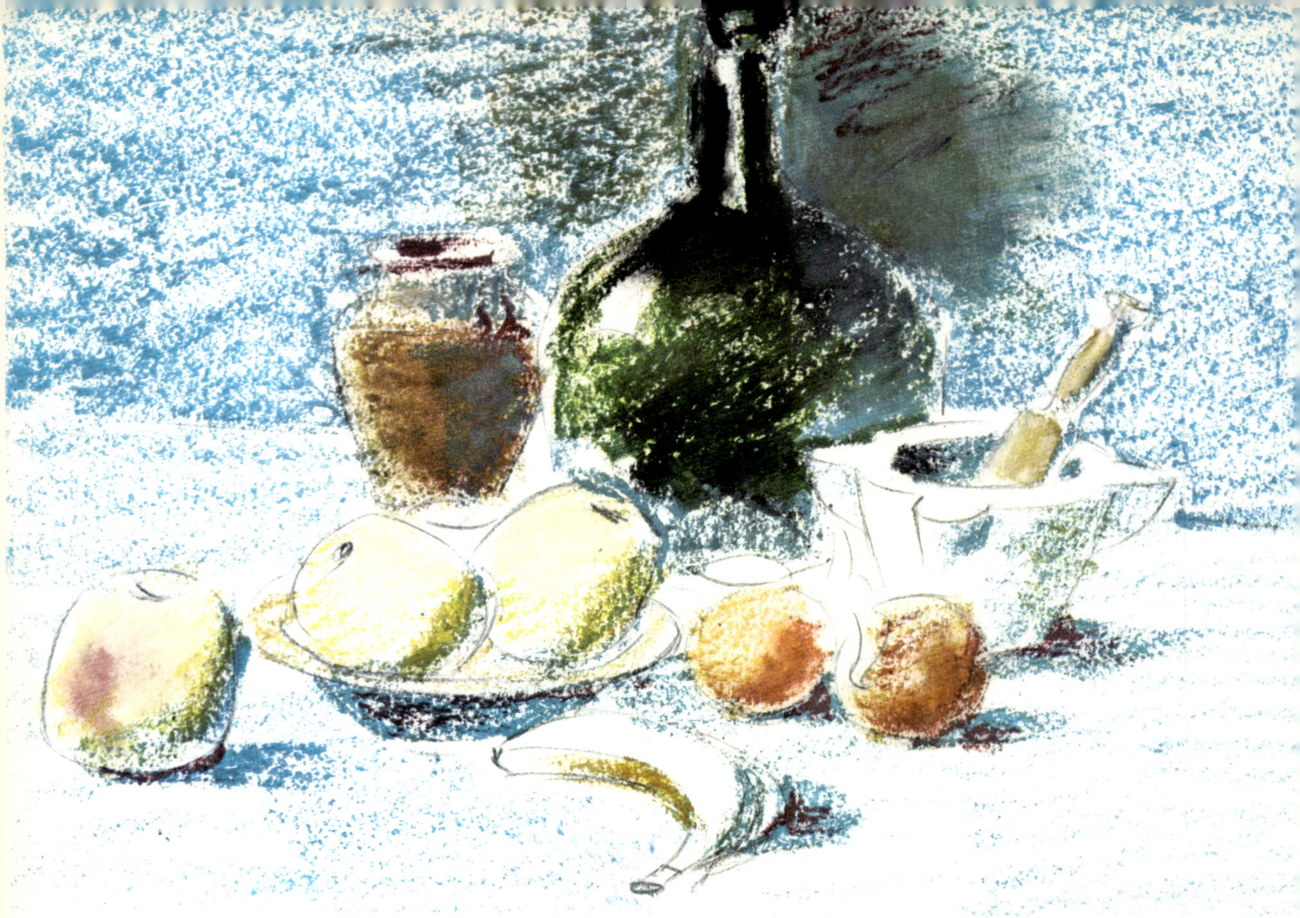

I began my painting by tracing in the background and the shaded parts in cyan blue. The shadowed area above the tablecloth is traced with slightly greater density. The white parts of the tablecloth are traced faintly with cyan blue. Black and green are used for the carafe and mixed with cyan blue to give a greyish effect. Ochre for the background and round the carafe. To the right, in the background, near the neck of the carafe, I added carmine and more cyan blue which is shaded off with my fingers. Leaving the carafe and turning to the pot I used ochre and burnt sienna and cyan blue for the shadows. I shaded off a little with my fingers — just a touch. For the apples I use yellow and this, with the cyan blue of the shadows gives too much green, so I add white. It's incredible how that merges with and harmonizes with the white. But the shaded parts are still too pale and need more working. I add a touch of carmine to the isolated apple on the left and shade it off. I consider a little pink, but it's not very satisfactory, so on to the oranges. I paint in orange and then add carmine to the parts in shadow, where I had already painted with cyan blue. Shaded off, this gives one a carmine-tinged brown, and so I leave it for the moment. Now a little ochre in the shaded part of the pestle and mortar, softening the highlights with white and merging both colours. The same ochre is used for the darker part of the banana. I use carmine to strengthen all the shadows projected on to the tablecloth.

I trace in the background with cyan blue and ochre which produces a dirty green. I add carmine more thickly, tone down and add a tiny bit of ultramarine, a little black

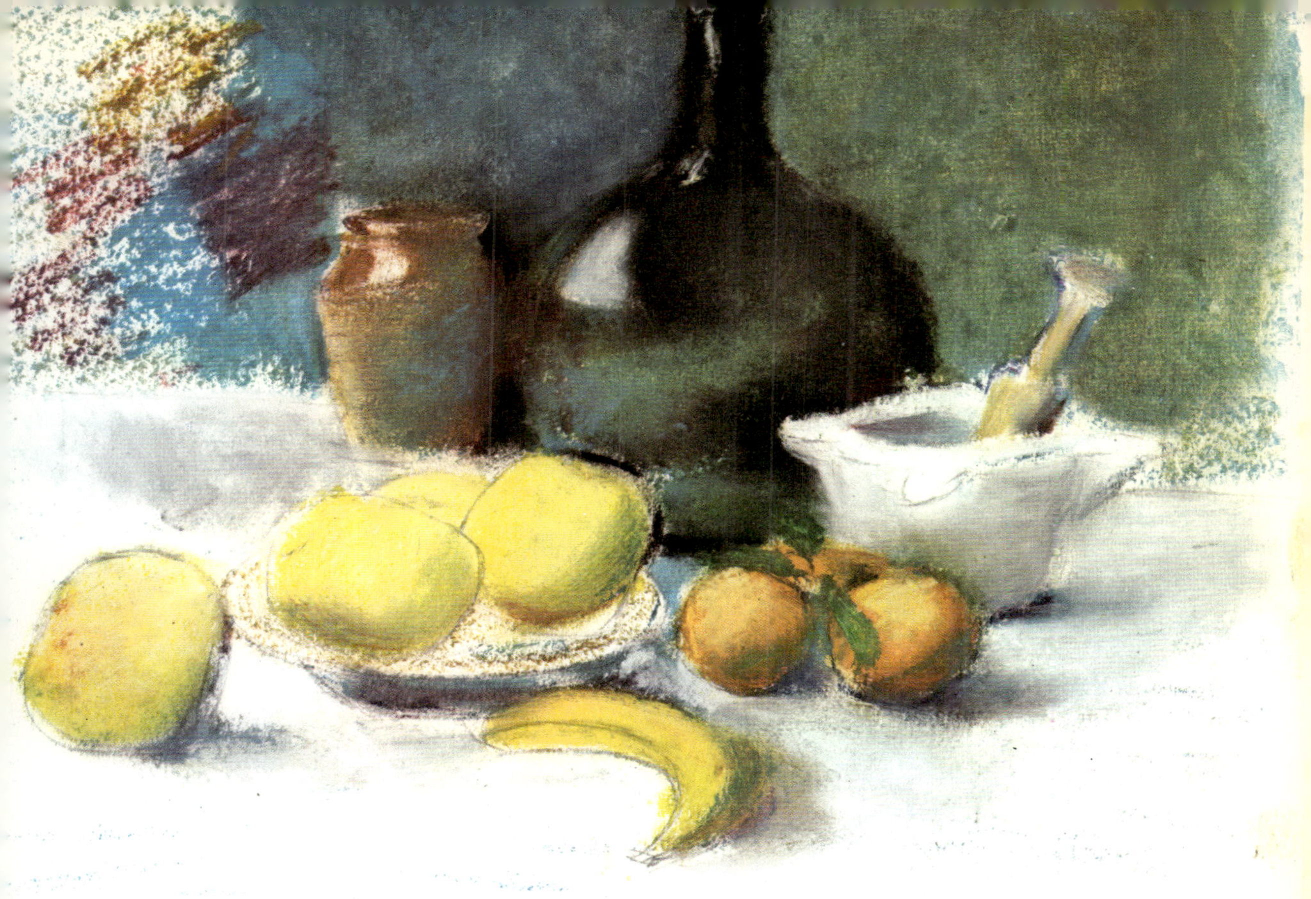

and some white. I tone down heavily, which leaves me with only a little paste. I need some more cyan blue and more white. Then for the same colours and green and a fair amount of black in the carafe. In the first stage I postponed putting in the whites of the carafe, but now, by intensifying and dimming its colouring, these whites are shown too sharply. I smear these highlights with white and also with the colours covering the tips of my fingers. The result is a bluish grey, and that's good enough for the time being. I use white for the mortar, tone it down and then add some grey. Then I have more yellow and white, for the apples; for their shadows I need cyan blue and black and a little carmine. Returning to the pestle, I use ochre and a little orange and white mixed up with the other colours because the space is too small for my fingers. I add cyan blue and carmine to the shadow of this mortar and move on to the oranges. I use orange, carmine and yellow and cyan blue for the shadows. I make a faint outline in black — I often have to tone it down, smearing with a cloth.

More colour, more paste and more depth, especially in the background to thin out shapes and outlines. I need ochre and burnt sienna for the pot and a little white to get more paste; also some cyan blue for the reflection of the shadow. I use black and cyan blue and green and ultramarine, but above all, black and green in the carafe. Now it's easy to create a patch of white in the bright part of the carafe; this is a satisfying thing

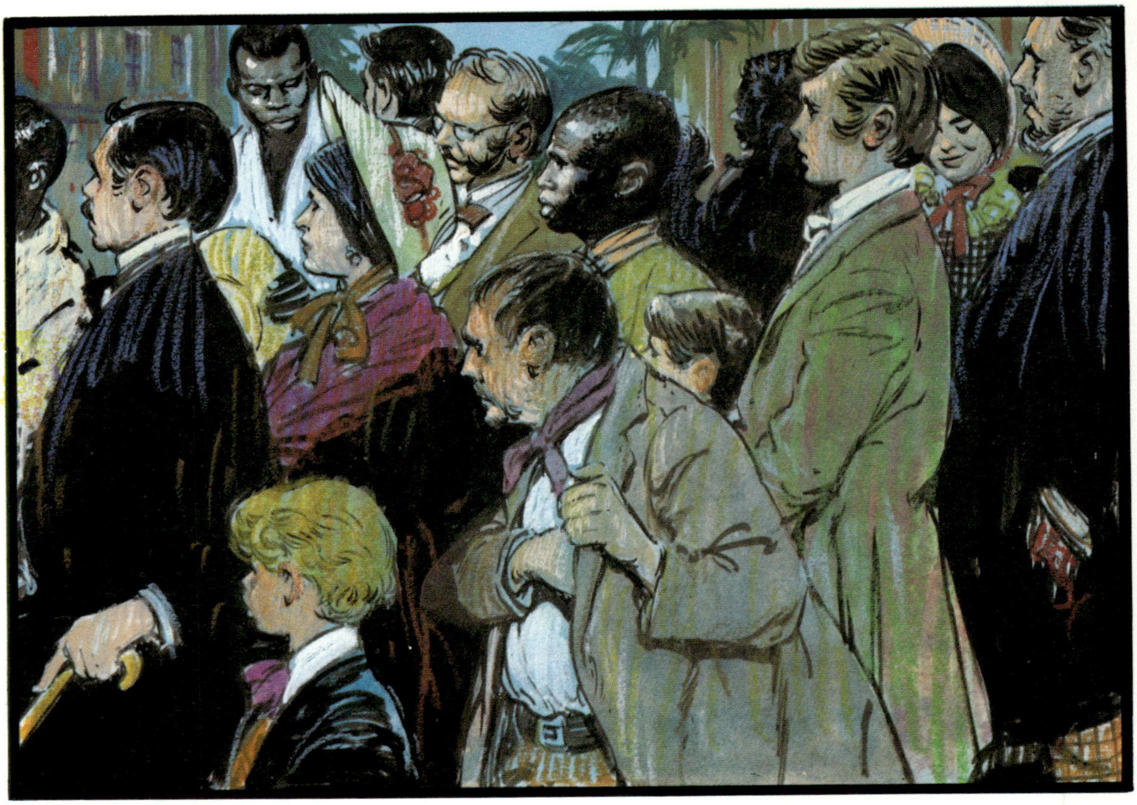

In tempera there is more colour and more earth. A sample of tempera colouring, although heavily diluted with water, always has an earthy, opaque, shrouding appearance.

Painting with light colours over dark

This explains how, using tempera, you can cover dark colours with light colours owing to tempera's covering potential. When painting in tempera, it is perfectly possible to execute a stroke in white over a black background.

Of course, to achieve this, the tempera paint must be diluted with very little water to produce a liquid paste which is slightly coagulated.

The affinity between the systems of tempera painting and watercolour painting makes it possible for both mediums to be used in a single work. It is usual, for example, in the field of illustrating, to use watercolours mixed with a small quantity of tempera or with tempera alone.

Dries quickly; tones dull once the paint is dry; matt appearance

Tempera painting dries fairly quickly. While the paint is still wet the colour is more intense and vivid than later after it has dried. It then has a notably matt appearance.

Tempera colours are obtainable in tubes and small glass jars. The colour, as it comes out of the tube or on opening the jar, has the appearance of a rather thick paste. There is really no difference between the two methods of packaging except that the paint contained in jars tends to dry more easily, for the obvious reason that it is more exposed to the air. In general, tempera in tubes is more suitable for painting in the open air, as it allows for greater proportioning on the plane of work similar to oil painting. The paint in jars is more suitable for work in the studio, and is generally used by commercial artists.

Obtainable in tubes and glass jars

The intensity, delicacy and stability of the colour (the fact that the colour is less lowered in tone once it is dry) is characteristic of the good foreign brands such as *Académie, Talens, Watteau, Pelikan, Paillard,* etc., with which you can be sure of a maximum yield of colour and opacity.

Brands

Brushes used for tempera painting are the same as those used for watercolour; the best are made from Kolinsky sable hair.

Brushes

Tempera painting can be applied on any surface: paper, canvas (with plenty of sizing), wood, whitewashed walls, glass, etc.; it requires only a minimum of preparation or priming for the colour to be more permanent and stable. You can paint on a whitewashed wall, for example, by preparing the surface beforehand with a very liquid layer of carpenter's glue which plugs the pores and prevents the plaster from sucking up the colour. But the most generally used medium is good quality drawing paper, especially light-grained Canson-type paper thick enough not to go out of shape of wrinkle up when wet paint is applied.

Cartridge paper is most commonly used

Tempera painting is used by many professional artists, mainly for painting landscapes. It is also used for schemes for architecture and design as well as plans for mural painting, a subject in which tempera is absolutely necessary for showing the matt qualities of paintings which are then made in distemper, with egg or with tempera itself. But tempera painting is most often applied in commercial art and advertising.

Potential

FROM THEORY TO PRACTICE

The technique in tempera painting is governed by the following factors characteristic of this medium: a) the fact that tempera paint is laid on thickly; b) its relatively rapid drying and c) the fact that the tone decreases once it is dry.

Three basic factors which govern the medium

We'll start by considering the influence of these three factors in the painting of a plain, wide background, painted with a composite colour, e.g. a bluish grey.

Problems in painting the background

In principle, the painting of a background like the one described seems to amount to making up the colour and applying it over white paper using a thick brush. But in practice, things like the following could happen: the colour is too thick and dries too quickly, making a hard task of spreading it out regularly. On the other hand, the colour may be too liquid so that traces of the brushes are left after the paint has dried; or the thickness of the paint is right, but the paint's distribution with the brush is not uniform, so that an excess of colour is deposited in some places, while others are left almost bare and, when the paint is dry, this gives rise to differences in tone. The final result will always be approximately the same. After the background is dry, patches and irregularities will appear in it, with some areas being darker than others.

Retouching is difficult

If you try later to retouch by using strokes or layers of paint in these irregular areas, the cure is worse than the disease. When these repainted parts have dried they, in their turn present problems similar to those left by poor-quality stain-remover on cloth — a sort of circle of a lighter tone — or else they have the appearance of ordinary patches of a darker colour than the background. If the colouring has all been used up and fresh colour has to be compounded, the matter is still more complicated. Whether you paint in watercolour, pastel or oils, it is difficult, almost impossible, for a second application of compounded colour (such as the bluish grey of the previous example) to present a tone identical with the first. This difficulty is increased when you paint with tempera colours, because the first layer of paint, once dried, clearly diminishes the tone — a minimum of 10 per cent for certain colours and up to 20 and 30 per cent in the purple and carmine of certain brands.

HOW TO PAINT AN EVEN BACKGROUND USING TEMPERA

The task of painting an even background with tempera is an everyday thing in commercial art — for posters, for example. Tempera is sometimes used for ordinary painting, especially in modern painting. In any event, these instructions apply to the technique of using tempera in general.

First of all you need to prepare enough colour. For making this compound and mixing the colours into a paste, the professional uses a wide, deep glass or china container.

MOUNTING THE DRAWING PAPER FOR PAINTING IN TEMPERA

When you paint in tempera on paper, the moisture finally causes the paper to lose its flatness. To avoid this mishap, which can actually do damage to the final painting, you have to have the paper mounted and tightly fixed, as shown below:

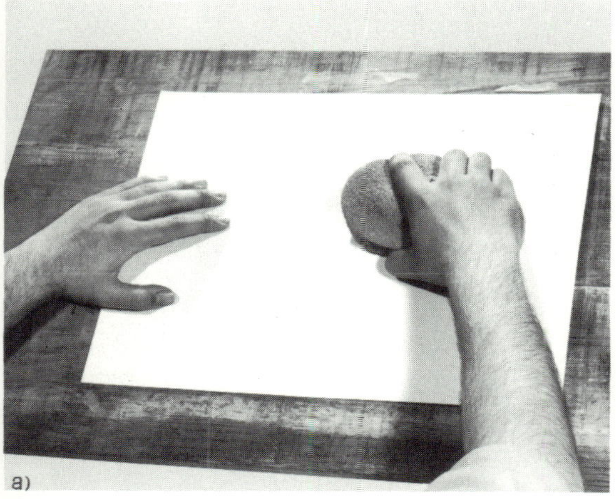

a)

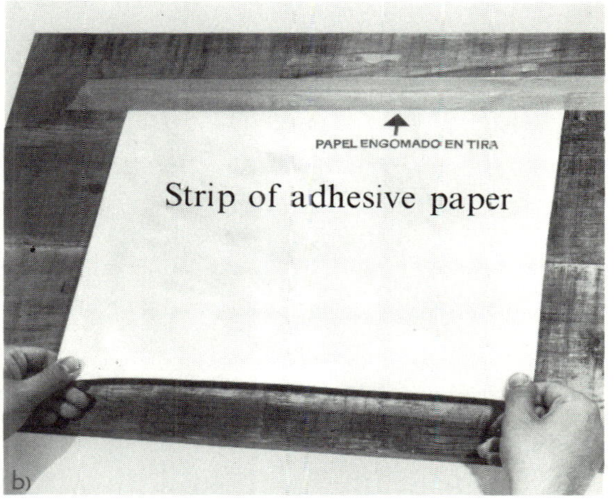

b)

a) Using a sponge lightly soaked in clear water, you moisten the drawing paper on one side only, without rubbing. Do this several times until the grain of the paper loses its usual stiffness.

b) Place the sheet of paper on a piece of wood and fasten one edge with a strip of adhesive paper.

Pull the paper gently and carefully to stretch it out and stick down this edge too with another strip of adhesive paper.

c) Finish off the mounting by sticking down the other two edges with adhesive paper, and leave the paper to dry, keeping it in a horizontal position. When the paper is dry, it stays taut and you can paint on it without its wrinkling up.

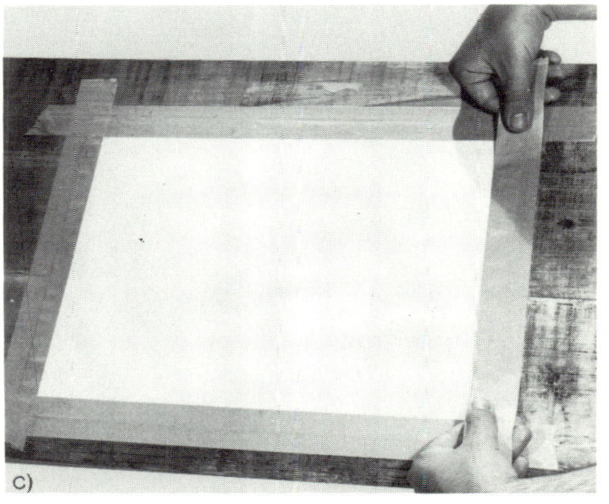

c)

The density of the mixture depends upon the quantity of water added to the colour. Generally speaking, just a few drops are enough for diluting the colour and forming a kind of liquid paste.

Not much water needed

The painting of a background is generally carried out with a special flat squirrel or nylon wash brush (available in sizes 1/2" to 4"). When the background is very large (the background of a poster, for example), a sponge roller is used.

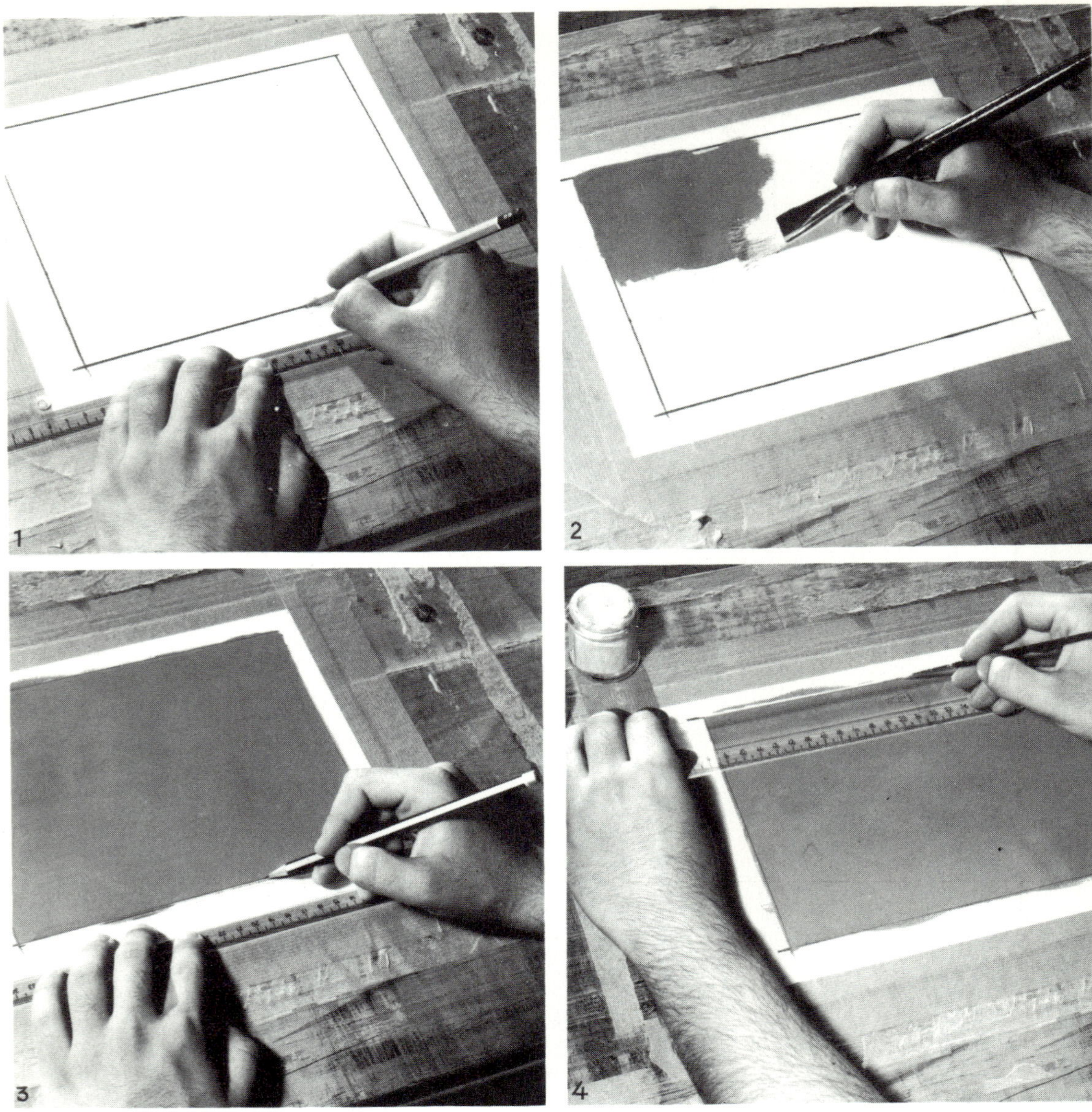

You then begin the painting with horizontal brush strokes. You cover the whole surface and spread the colour out quite uniformly, working very quickly so that the whole background is wet when you finish, avoiding going over the lower part when the upper part has already dried. It is sometimes necessary to go over the first areas again before you've got to the last sections.

Then you apply a second layer, while the background is still wet, now painting with vertical strokes. At this stage the paper now begins to absorb the moisture, so that it is easy to preserve it.

A third coat may be necessary. In any event, lastly, it is as well to give a patina to the colour — to pass the brush over it gently, and smooth and spread out the tempera, eliminating any marks made by the brush hairs (these marks make a kind of furrow which can alter the tone once the background is dry).

When working in these conditions, don't paint the background within given limits, i.e., within a previously drawn square or rectangle. The usual method is a follows: 1. Draw in the borders of the background in pencil, pressing hard so that the lines are visible while you are painting the first coats; 2. Paint overlapping the edges; 3. Draw the borders of the background again in pencil, after the tempera has dried; 4. Cover the edges with white tempera or, in cases where the background is small, cut it down with scissors and fix it on to a fresh piece of paper or white frame.

Bordering a background

If, in spite of everything, the background is still faulty, you can try and rescue it, first, with a slightly damp coat of colour which dampens the previous painting, and then with normal coats, repeating the process.

When a background is dry and finished, take care to protect it from possible accidents. A drop of water, for example, is enough to bring the whole work to ruin.

Painting of graduations of light and shade

When the graduation of light and shade can be painted all at one go, by juxtaposing the two tones first, and then mixing and graduating then with the brush, and when you can carry this out while the paint is wet, there is no problem. When we turn from theory to practice later on, you'll paint some of these graduations more easily, even when painting with watercolours.

Difficulties arising from wet and dry paint

Well-known and numerous are the problems when the graduation forms part of a model, e.g. when, with a hasty or delicate graduation, you have to form a body, a head, and, for example, the passing from light to shade on a cheek, on the point of a chin, on a nose, etc. Because, of course, in cases like these it is not possible to paint the whole of the subject while still keeping the paint dry. It is natural that, when you are shaping (drawing and painting at the same time) the parts which are in shadow in an area should spring from those which were painted in another place. You can see that you may wish to strengthen or lighten a shade of colour when, once it is dry and graduated with another shade, you discover it needs more or less intensity. The problem then arises, simply, from the wish to graduate a dry area with a damp one. This is the great problem of the technique of tempera. Let me emphasize this:

The greatest problem in tempera painting arises from the need to graduate, in many cases, an area correctly drawn and painted and finished, which is therefore dry, with another area which is still free from paint or which, having been already painted, has to be altered.

For example, you are painting a head or a face. You begin the painting with the parts in shadow of the cheek. Quickly, without considering what follows, you compound the lightest colour corresponding to the illuminated areas of the face. With great care (still thanks to the operation performed while the paint of both areas was wet) carry on graduating the two tones. *But* you'll find you have a most beautiful neck to that head and this is linked to the face without any sign of transition. In this neck there are some shades which also need mixing and graduating with those of the point of the chin, the jaw, the ear, etc. And the colours of the point of the chin and below the ear are already dry. How can you graduate a dry area with a wet one?

PAINTING GRADUATIONS OF LIGHT AND SHADE WITH TEMPERA COLOURS

To start with, you need to divide the subject into graduated areas, sections whose edges needn't be merged because they already have one, or at most, two graduations of light and shade. This means you can devote your attention to a given area on which you can concentrate as well as keeping the juxtaposed tones damp and blending them easily with your brush.

Division of the subject into graduated areas

Brush mixing is a special technique. It involves "combing out" the different colours with a scarcely damp brush, so that the bristles can be used like a comb. It's easy if you attack it like this: first paint the two tones or colours whose edges have to be mixed. Then, taking one of the two colours on the brush, mix and blend and merge it into the other with horizontal or vertical strokes, depending on what you are painting.

Combing the background

You probably won't achieve a perfect graduation just yet and to carry on harmonizing the edges with the whole, you then go on to "combing" the graduated area, like this:

Without washing the brush, wring it out with the rag and squeeze it with the thumb and forefinger to flatten the end and separate the hairs by the smallest fraction, so that their position reminds one of that of the teeth of a very fine comb. Pass this

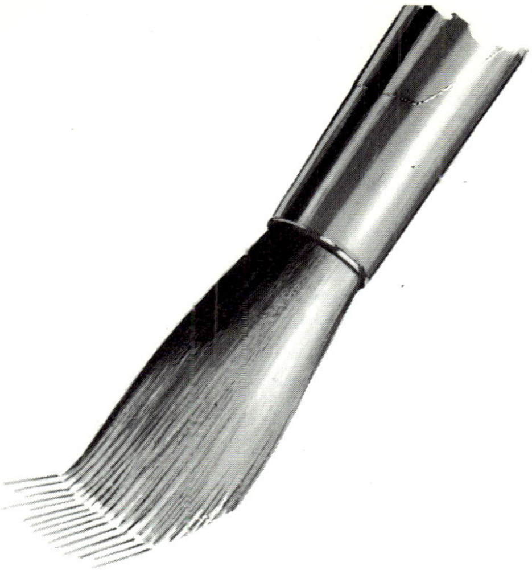

Here, enlarged, we show the end of a brush, which, after being flattened and arranged with the fingers, is prepared for "combing" an area with tempera and so helping to construct a graduation, whether on a wet or dry area.

"comb" gently over the area to be merged, treating the colours which are still wet with great care, keeping the brush strokes going in the proper direction and transferring light colours to dark, and vice versa.

This is the way to merge light and shade when the colours can be kept wet.

If this chance has been lost, and you have to combine light and shade next to or with an area which is already dry, there are two ways of setting about it: a) you moisten the dry area with clear water and then go ahead graduating in the way described, or b), you paint in the graduation over the dry place, i.e. you take on a load of very thick paint on the brush and apply gentle strokes on the dry area.

How to graduate light and shade over a dry area

The first method is suitable for any type of merging. All you need to do is to moisten the dry area very carefully, using only a little water and with your brush in the "comb" form. You "comb" the area very gently in order to prevent the colours becoming loosened. This must be done without pressing and the moistening must be done with just one or two strokes of the brush.

The second method for merging colours over a dry surface is useful only for painting small graduations and for painting in areas where there is not much difficulty.

HOW TO RETOUCH COLOUR MERGING

In spite of all your care it is possible that, after the painted area is finished and dry, you may need to retouch or alter the way you have colour merged. It's quite common, for example, when everything's over, for one to find a fault in construction — a nose seems too broad, let's say, because the graduation from light to shadow has been slightly moved from one side to another.

Moving the position of a graduation system when dry or wet

In these, and in other, cases, we must distinguish between small alterations and important changes; between extending by a tiny amount, for example, the graduation which makes the nose, or making a major alteration to the whole shape of the nose (shadow, half-tones, highlights, etc). If the change is to be an important one you'll need to moisten the whole area with clear water and then paint again and go over the different tones. Sometimes this can be done successfully without adding any paint by "combing", but doing it simple with a moist brush; sometimes it may need the application of more colour. If the retouching is a minor one, you should just need to "comb" with the slightly damp brush, with light strokes over the dark area, taking colour from this area with gentle strokes, towards the light area, by extending or moving the merged tones, by shortening the graduation and making it softer — in a word, by painting, drawing and shaping.

Do yoy have to paint according to a preconceived ideal

From what we've been talking about you may think that the technique of tempera painting requires finishing according to a preconceived ideal — for instance, painting an eye and continuing painting that eye until it is complete. This is true, up to a point. The essentials of tempera — thick paint which dries quickly and alloys the tone — require a rapid and almost finalized decision according to a preconceived notion. But you need to differentiate between an artistic and commercial style of painting.

The artistic style

At the outset, it is almost always possible to paint without achieving a complete merging of the tones; a perfectly harmonized graduation will not be suitable for a landscape or a still-life painted on an aesthetic level. In general, the really skilled artist paints better with even colours and with superimposed brush strokes creating an optical feeling of blending. In non-commercial painting with tempera you can work in stages as when you are working in watercolour or oils. In practice, a landscape painted in tempera will not differ much from a landscape painted in watercolour or in oils.

The commercial or publicity style

For publicity or commercial art, however, you'll have to cover subjects, like the illustration used in the frontispiece, which can be achieved with the fluency and spontaneity of a good artist. But in other cases, where the subject demands a more detailed finishing, then you really do need to have to do the job by areas, and it can be finished only after last-minute retouching.

TEMPERA: FROM THEORY TO PRACTICE

BLACK AND WHITE PAINTING OF A COWBOY'S HEAD

YOU WILL NEED: TEMPERA: WHITE; WATERCOLOUR; BLACK; PAPER — CARTRIDGE TYPE; BRUSHES — NOS. 2, 6 and 10; PIECE OF PAPER TO SERVE AS A PALETTE; A RAG FOR CLEANING THE BRUSHES; WATER; HB LEAD PENCIL; INDIARUBBER, RULER AND SET- SQUARE.

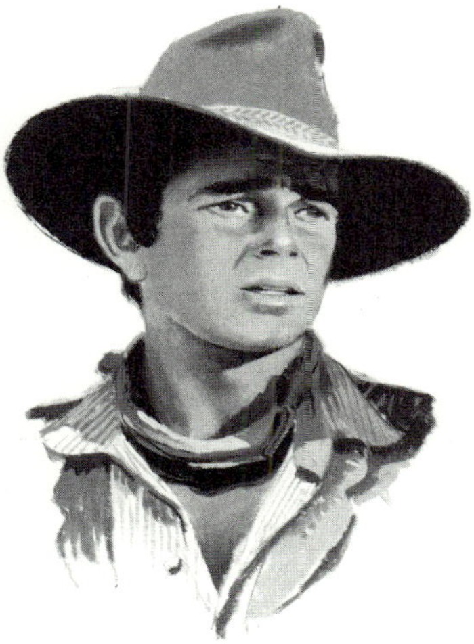

You may wonder why this exercise has been planned with white tempera and black watercolour, without other colours being used, but you've seen that tempera painting calls for a complicated technique. We'll keep to black and white for the moment. But experimenting and working in black and white means that you must concentrate on overcoming the difficulties created by graduations, and harmonizing on dry or wet paper.

There is a good reason for using black watercolour instead of black tempera: tempera, mixed with watercolours, does not decrease the tones so much.

In spite of these simplifications, the exercise is a difficult one, so we'll start easily, with a rough light sketch which should be useful when you come to the final exercise.

To acquire some basic knowledge, begin by painting the figures on the following pages with (A, B and C) a graduation painted when wet, and in D and E, a graduation painted when dry. F, G and H show a graduation applied to the form of a sphere, and I to M, various graduations applied to a cylindrical form.

For this, use a sheet of paper of best quality thick drawing paper.

A

B

C

First exercises

Materials

Get your gear ready. You'll need a drawing table propped up or placed against the table at a slight angle like a writing desk. You'll need plenty of water, preferably in two jars — one for washing and the other for rinsing and moistening, bearing in mind that tempera smears much more than watercolour. Then you need a piece of thick drawing paper to serve as a palette for composing the mixtures and tones. The two brushes and the rag are for drying and draining off.

Encasing of the shapes

Draw Figs. C, D and M with an HB pencil, using a ruler and set-square. Also draw the circle corresponding to the figure of the sphere. Make all these figures the same size as shown here.

Take on 1.5 centimetres of white paste for .5 centimetre of black watercolour

Finally, put some white and black on the paper palette. This is where you have to be careful. You always have to rely on a greater quantity of white than of black. The colour white, as we shall see later, is used up in much greater quantity than black. To get a medium grey, you need three to four times more white than black.

PAINTING WITH A MOIST GRADUATION (A, B, C).

Fill your No. 2 brush with clean water and add this amount (no more for the moment) to the white. Dilute the white in this small amount of water. It should be enough to obtain a thick paste, but fluid enough for the paint to run easily. Bear in mind that the thickness has to cover the pencil outlines.

Paint approximately three-quarters of the graduation in white, as you can see in Fig. A.

System to be followed for painting a moist graduation

Wash the brush; rinse it out as quickly as you can and apply it, when it is almost dried out, to the portion of black watercolour, making the paint into paste (you have to make an equally thick paste). Now paint the lefthand side until it is joined up with the previous white. Now, moving quickly, paint the black towards the white and back again to the black (B).

Now take the No. 10 brush. Moisten it and dry it out on the rag, flattening down the end of it to form a "comb". Then try to harmonize with very gentle vertical brush strokes, using the tip of the brush and working from left to right and back again. Notice that the black greatly influences the white and take care that you don't go too far and get a complete black. You may need to take on a little more white or black. Don't worry about going over the edges.

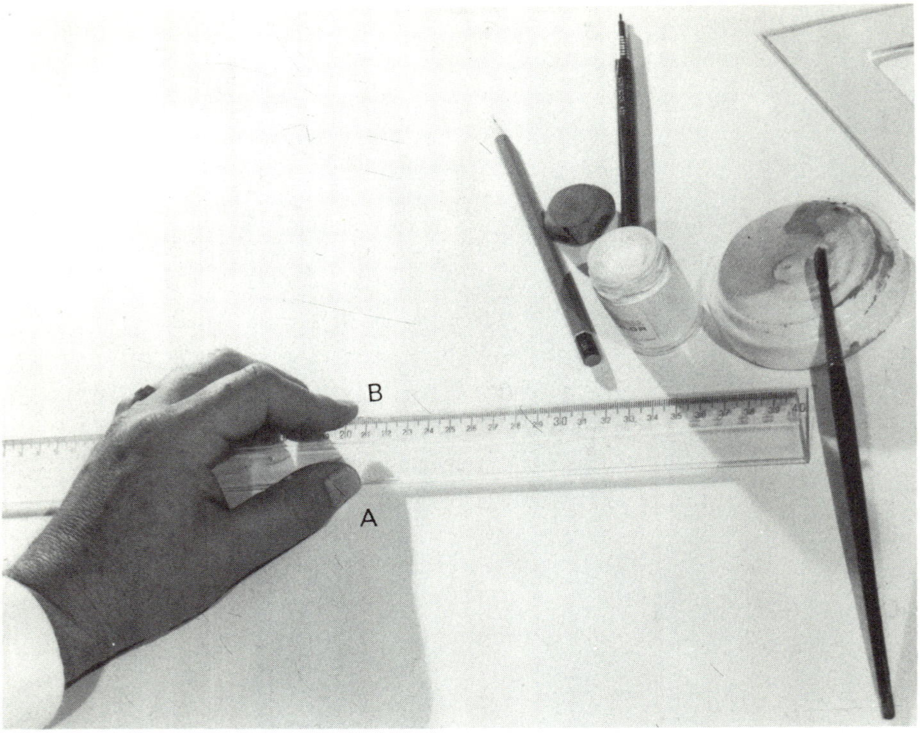

I

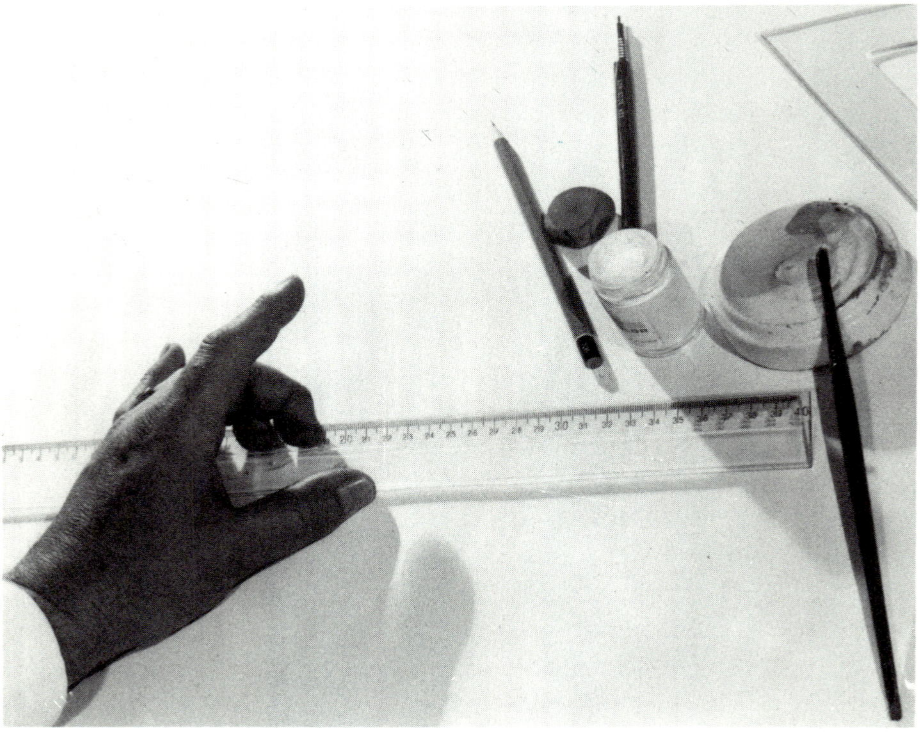

II

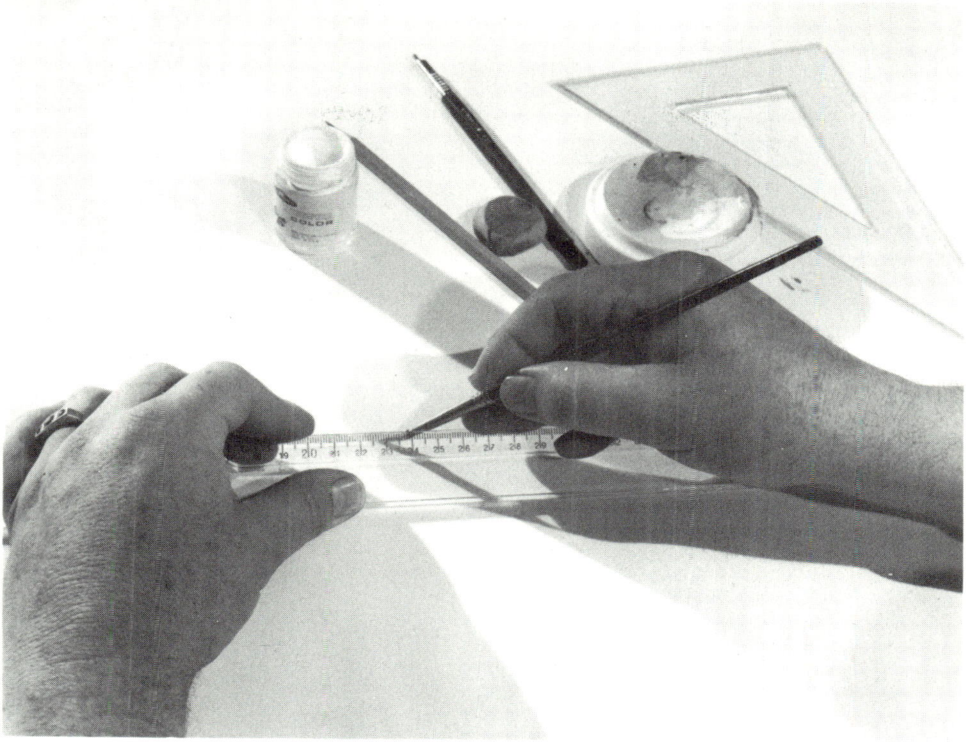

III

RULER METHOD (SEE OVERLEAF)

I. Take the ruler in your left hand as shown in the illustration opposite. Your thumb holds the edge A firmly down on the surface, while the middle finger raises edge B, thus forming a wedge. At the same time, the index finger presses this same edge B downwards, so that the ruler stays fixed at a slope; the fourth finger and the little finger help by pressing and raising to form a lever.

II. Once the ruler is in position, take the brushful of white tempera, holding it in a more frontal position than usual, keeping the ends of the fourth and little fingers under the edge of the ruler, keeping those fingers firmly in place rigidly so that the end of the ruler is always at the same level.

III. Now it's a question of graduating the level we spoke of; the end of the brush touches and paints (while you bend slightly forward) the paper or surface on which the ruler rests. It will be enough to let the hand slip along the ruler from left to right to finish off the painting with thick rectilineal strokes.

PAINTING OF DRY GRADUATION (D, E)

System to follow when painting a "dry" graduation

Within a rectangle measuring approximately the same as Fig. D, first paint in a medium grey to more or less cover half. Then paint the other half black. Wait until both tones have completely dried and shade them by the two systems previously explained: a) for the lower part, moisten the grey and black and blend them with the brush, as you do when you work "moist"; b) for the upper part, graduate "dry", by superimposing very light strokes of black over grey, painting with the brush in the "comb" shape, etc.

Once both graduations have been finished, separate them with a white stripe drawn with the brush, using the ruler and painting with the brush propped up as described on previous page.

PAINTING OF GRADUATIONS APPLIED IN THE FORM OF A SPHERE (F, G, H)

Draw the sphere with ordinary pencil, with a finish as shown in Figure F, showing the play of light and shade.

Painting the graduations which form a sphere

Working as quickly as possible, paint in the three circular tones or strips (a, b, c) corresponding to the "hump" of the shadow, the intermediate shadow and the reflected light. Then, working quickly to paint with all the tones moist, paint the light part with the light green, leaving the shining part in the upper middle section. Use a No. 2 brush. Now take a No. 10 brush, moisten it, flatten the end so as to form a "comb", and blend the tones which form the sphere, until you achieve a perfect *circular graduation,* as shown in Figure H.

Then paint in pure white the shining part in the upper section. If the light grey of the light part is already dry, create this shining point by "dry" graduation, by painting with the brush in the "comb" form, taking a tiny amount of fairly liquid white and shading off with a series of very small strokes.

Paint the shadow cast on to the ground in dark grey, slightly lighter on the left foreground, and end the exercise by removing, with white, the bits which have gone over the edges. Use this final retouch to shade off these outlines slightly, creating a feeling of atmosphere (see Fig. H).

D

E

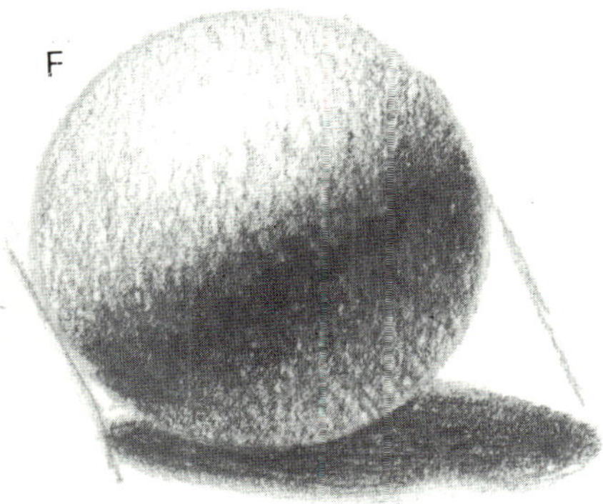

F

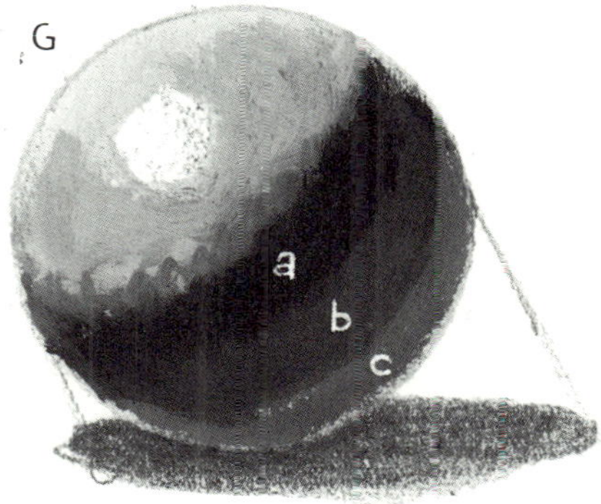

G

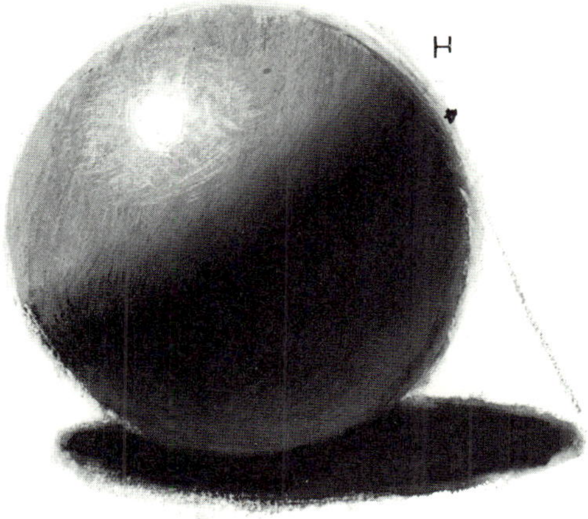

H

PAINTING VARIOUS GRADUATIONS APPLIED TO A CYLINDRICAL FORM

Paint a white strip.

Graduate this white stroke and blend it with the previous greys. You use the same No. 2 brush for this (Fig. J).

Paint a black strip on the right side. Graduate it with the previous grey (Fig. K).

Finally, paint a light grey strip, corresponding to the reflected light of the cylinder (Fig. L).

Process to be followed for painting graduations for shaping a cylindrical form.

Now use the system of painting tempera strips with the ruler previously described and pass over the No. 2 or No. 4 brush once or twice. Doing this will graduate the latter grey of the reflected light, harmonize the width and blending of the other graduations. Repaint and retouch. The last task is to apply the final touches — this may take up some time; you may find you need to add white, grey or black.

Don't worry whether you go over the edges. If the brush strokes go too far you can simply retouch and prune away with white, as in the last Fig. M.

Once the pruning with white has been completed, draw and paint the cavity in the upper part and its edges. This final part is painted over the previous part. This is one of the great advantages of tempera: its covering quality allows you to paint and repaint over what has already been painted.

NOW THE DEFINITIVE EXERCISE

Pass on to the final exercise: painting the head of a cowboy

This consists of painting, in black watercolour and white tempera. Our subject is the portrait of the cowboy reproduced on the photograph on page 77. So that this exercise can be more effective, it's a good idea to make an experimental test, as a professional would do if he were commissioned to do a frontispiece or an illustration like this. To get better results with the examples which illustrate this lesson, begin by painting an experimental draft which will enable you to reach a better result in the final illustration. Use the following exercise for painting the head as an experiment, a study in advance, using the same process with which you can paint the final picture.

Size — 11 cms from the top of the hat to the tip of the chin

Work to a size approximately the same as the figure on the following page, i.e., paint the head about 11 cms high, taking this dimension from the top of the hat to the tip of the chin.

STAGE 1. USE PENCIL FOR CONSTRUCTION AND BASIC SHADING

Working with an ordinary HB pencil, set down the subject on the scale suggested above.

Important: you are making an *illustration,* a picture which might be used for the frontispiece of a novel or for illustrating a magazine story. The professional illustrator also makes use of photos taken mainly from cinema stills or from photos used in the advertising of a film. He doesn't paint a portrait, but an anonymous face, i.e. he doesn't care about reproducing a likeness. So remember that:

In an illustration of this kind it isn't necessary to achieve a likeness

You aren't painting the portrait of a particular film star, but the face of any cowboy you like, not of any special person.

Then try to construct, taking care with your proportions, the position of the components which make up the face. Paint a well-constructed head, but not a portrait; it's not necessary to copy the photo in an effort to attain a likeness. In fact do it freehand, at sight, in the hope that you'll produce an anonymous face.

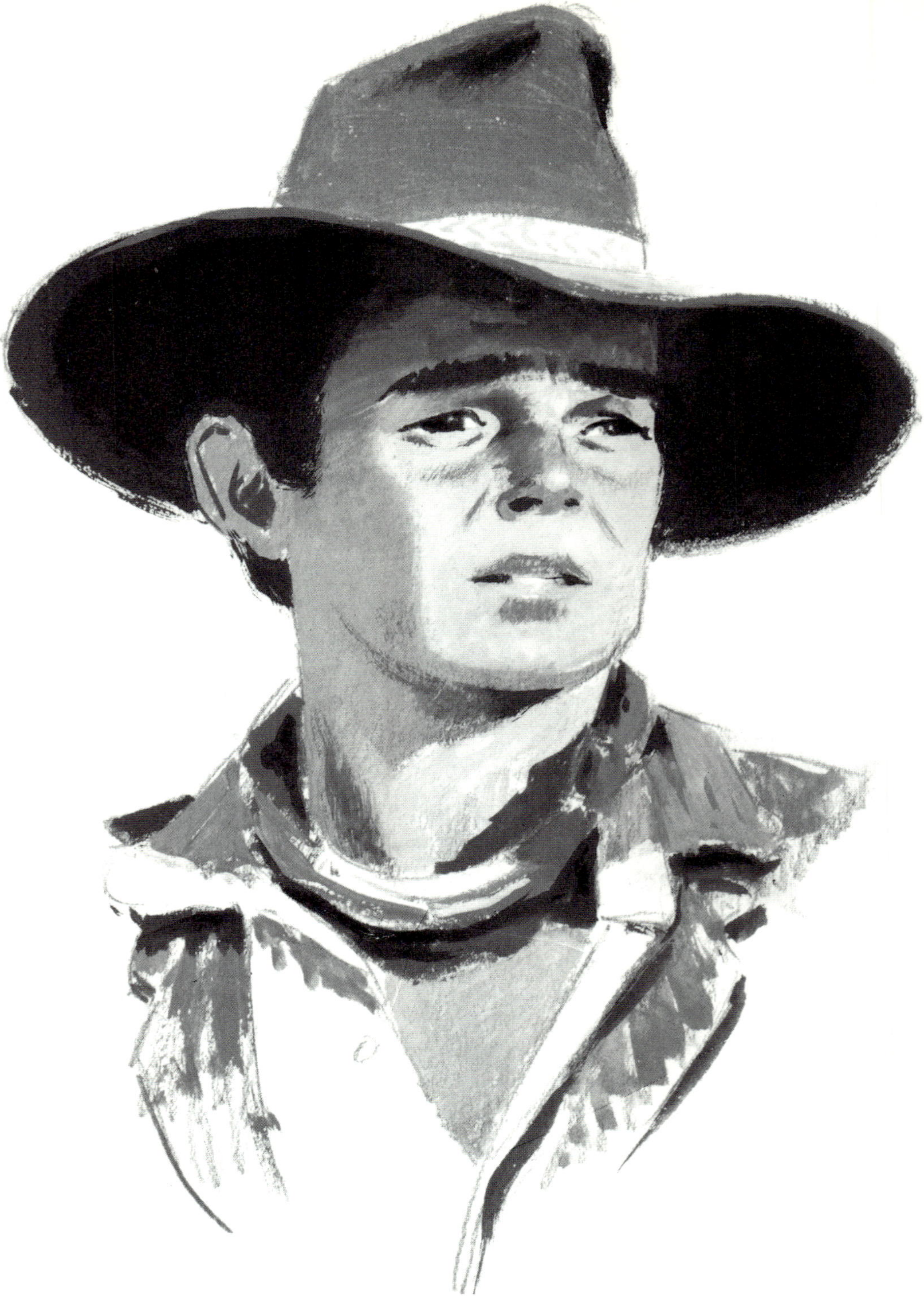

PREVIOUS STUDY. I made this sketch myself to give you a better estimate of the difficulties respecting the graduations which form the face; at the same time I made a first study of the tones. You'll notice that these tones are quite separate — compare this picture with Fig. F.

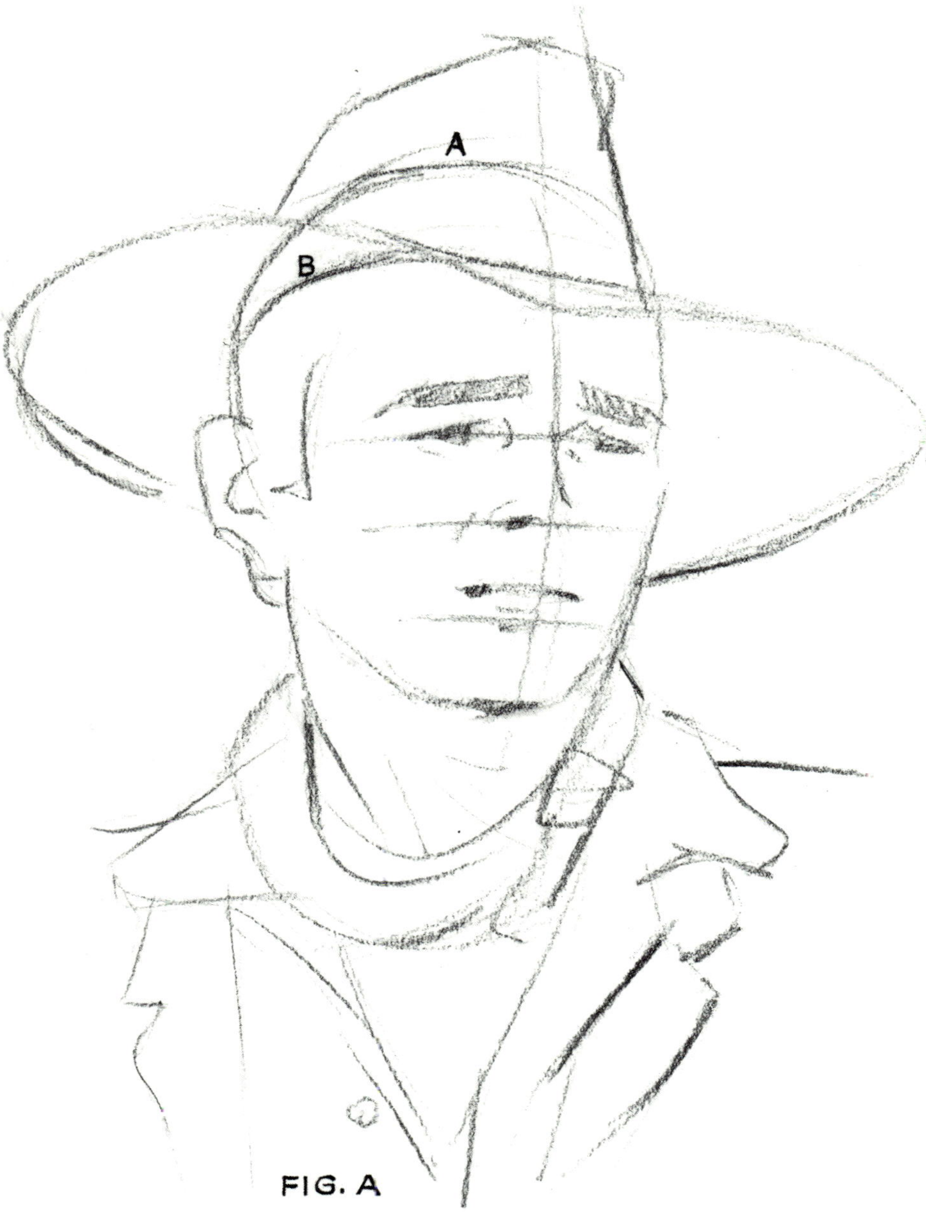

FIG. A

For this stage, see Fig. A above; it's reproduced on a smaller scale to fit the book. You'll see that, in this first draft, I've drawn the upper outline of the face, imagining the outline of the hollow of the hat (lines A and B). Also note that, across the eyes, and under the nose and mouth, there are some slightly curved horizontal lines on a vertical axis. This helps check proportions and dimensions. You do the same, to be certain of a quicker and more accurate sketch.

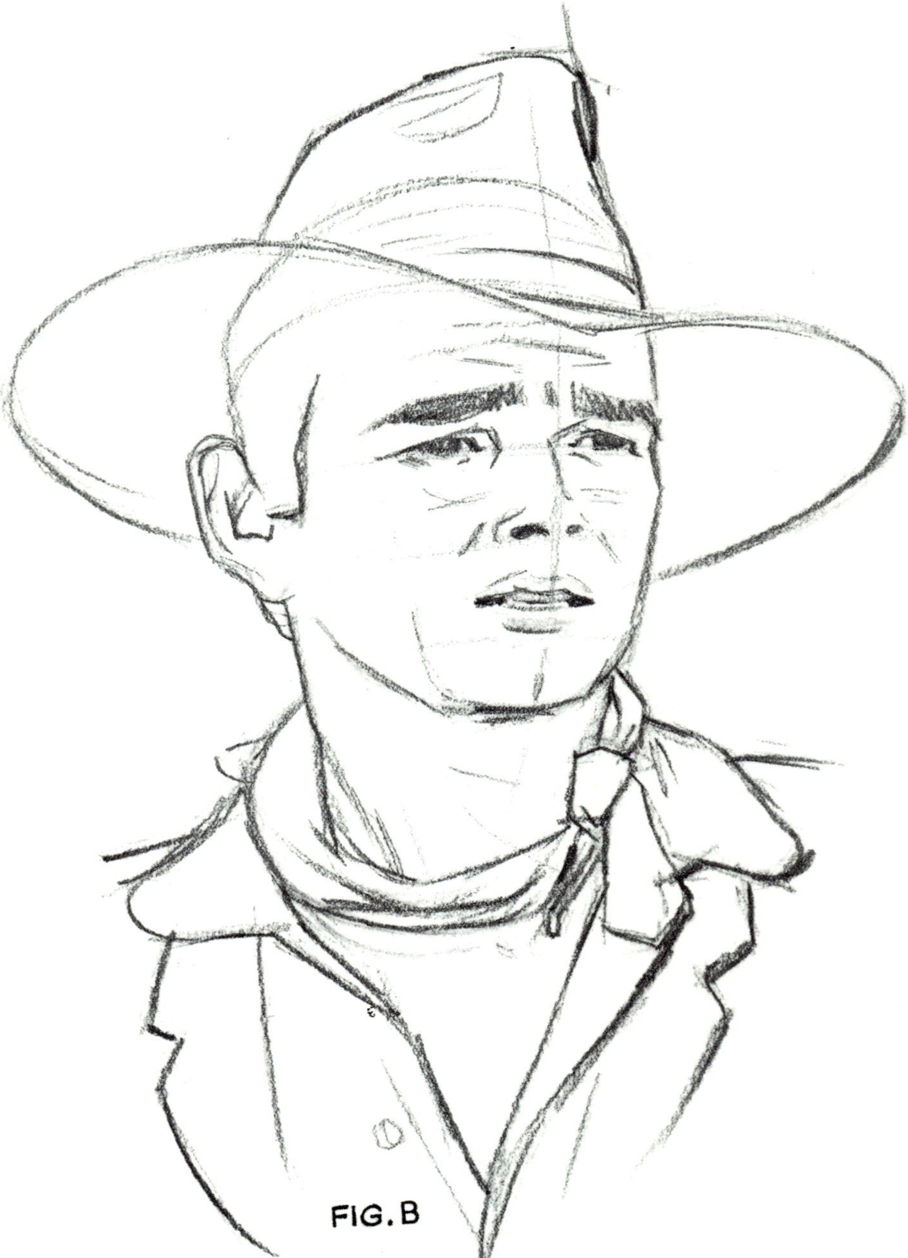

FIG. B

Then intensify the original sketch and put in details, drawing in the lines, finishing as far as possible the basic construction of the head and chest. Draw harder, as if you were in the final stages. (Fig. B).

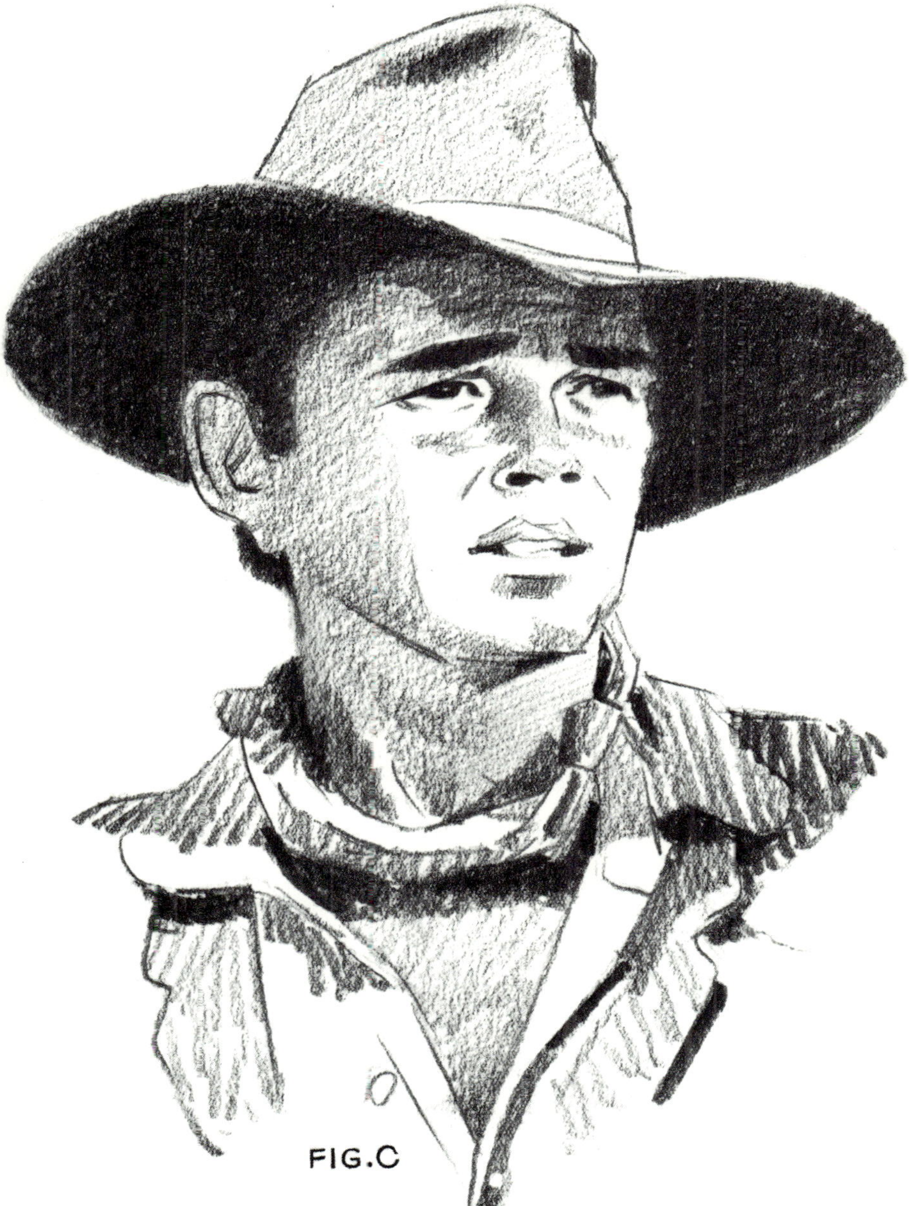

FIG. C

Then go ahead and estimate the play of light and shade, drawing, putting in grey tones and shading vigorously. This almost final sketch will help you with the next (Fig. C).

STAGE II: GENERAL MODULATION WHEN USING TEMPERA

Begin by painting in the black of the brim of the hat. Then go on with the grey which forms the shaded part ot the cheek, point of the chin and part of the neck. Notice that the edge of this shadow has been graduated "dry", by applying the brush with very little, but very thick paint, and by the gentle treatment of the grain of the paper in order to achieve this "dry" graduation (Fig. D.)

System to be followed for a general modulation (Figs. D and E)

It is important that you should continue this grey of the cheek as far as the temple and above the eyebrow.

Paint quickly. While this grey is wet, construct the graduation which forms the shadow of the brim on the forehead. Then continue downwards from under the brim, to the brow, with a dark grey, almost black. Go on downwards, and add the light grey for the cheek, graduating and blending. Then try and form the slight tonal differences in the lines of the brow and the space between the eyebrows.

So far so good. Now paint the nose — the part of the nose in shadow — painting the inner graduations moist and the edges dry — (See Fig. D). Using the brush with only a little paint, and painting dry, construct the shadows below the nose and lips, using the same grey as you used for the cheek.

For Fig. E you have to do several things:

I. Paint the crown of the hat in a grey slightly darker than that used for the cheek;

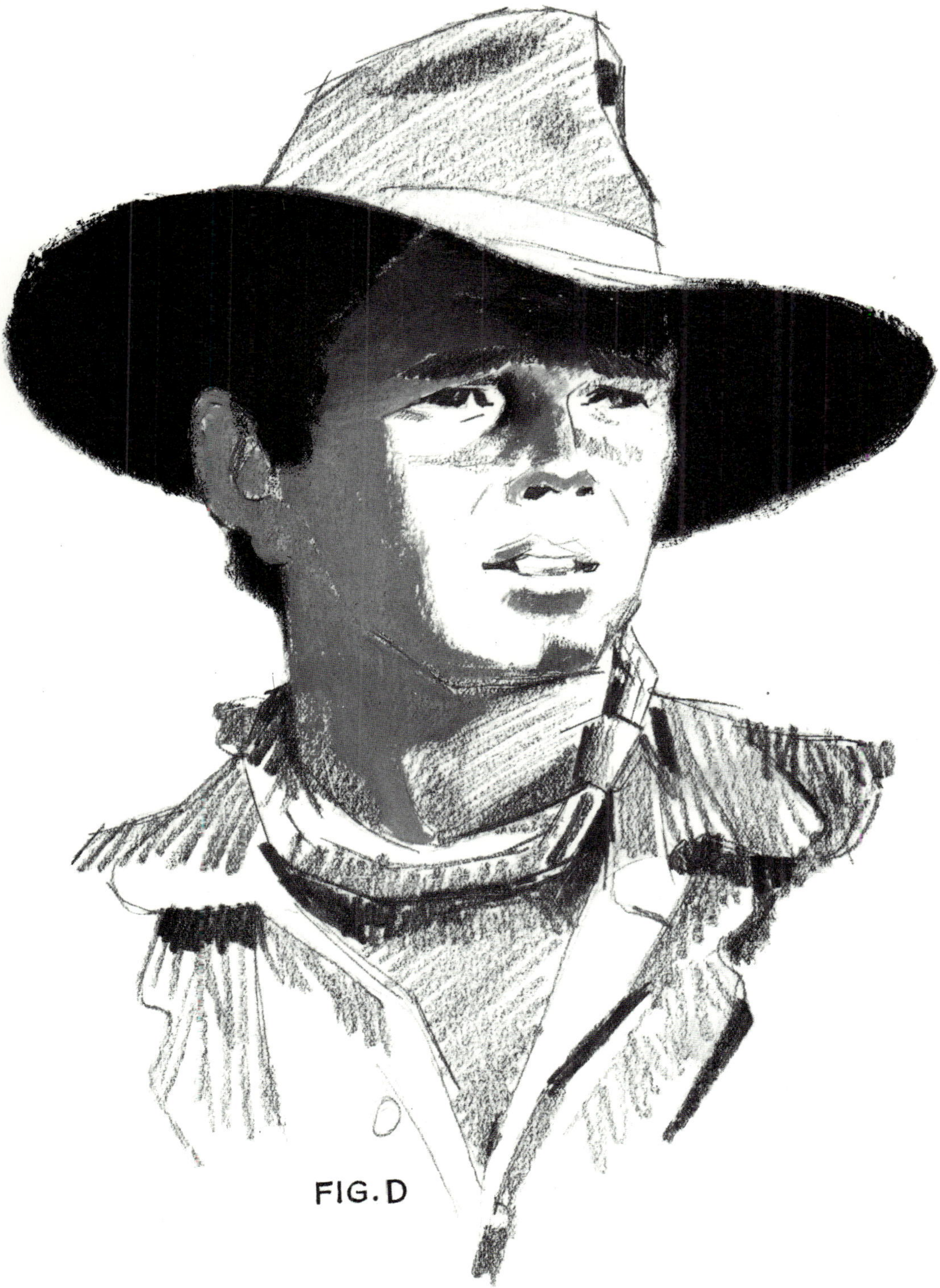

FIG. D

II. Paint, with the same grey which you used for the hat, the parts in shade of the handkerchief tied round the neck, and the part of the chest revealed by the open neck of the shirt;

III. Paint and form the highlighted parts of the face with a *very light grey,* and try to blend it into the edges of the parts in shadow; the cheek, tip of the chin, nose, etc. Notice that the whites of the eyes, the light patch at the end of the nose and on the lower lip stay as they are, without being painted;

IV. Paint and shape the highlighted part of the neck, graduating here by moistening the darker grey. Note that in the previous Fig. D, when painting the shadow of the cheek and neck, I have purposely left unpainted a very thin line corresponding to the line used for painting the jaw and the edge round the chin from ear to ear. This precaution forms a division of areas. It can be used later for graduating both the cheek and the neck, both parts being formed by the system of moistening areas which are already dry in order to blend them with wet, recently painted areas.

STAGE III: FINISHING OFF YOUR DRAWING

In this last stage, let us emphasize the aspects whose results you can see in Fig. F.

The order in which these instructions are given corresponds to the process you follow in Fig. F.

I. Eyebrows: painted and "combed" with the tip of a flattened brush forming the "comb". Draw them at the same time, and graduate them at the extremities; then apply a slightly lighter grey.

II. The space between the eyebrows and the upper part of the

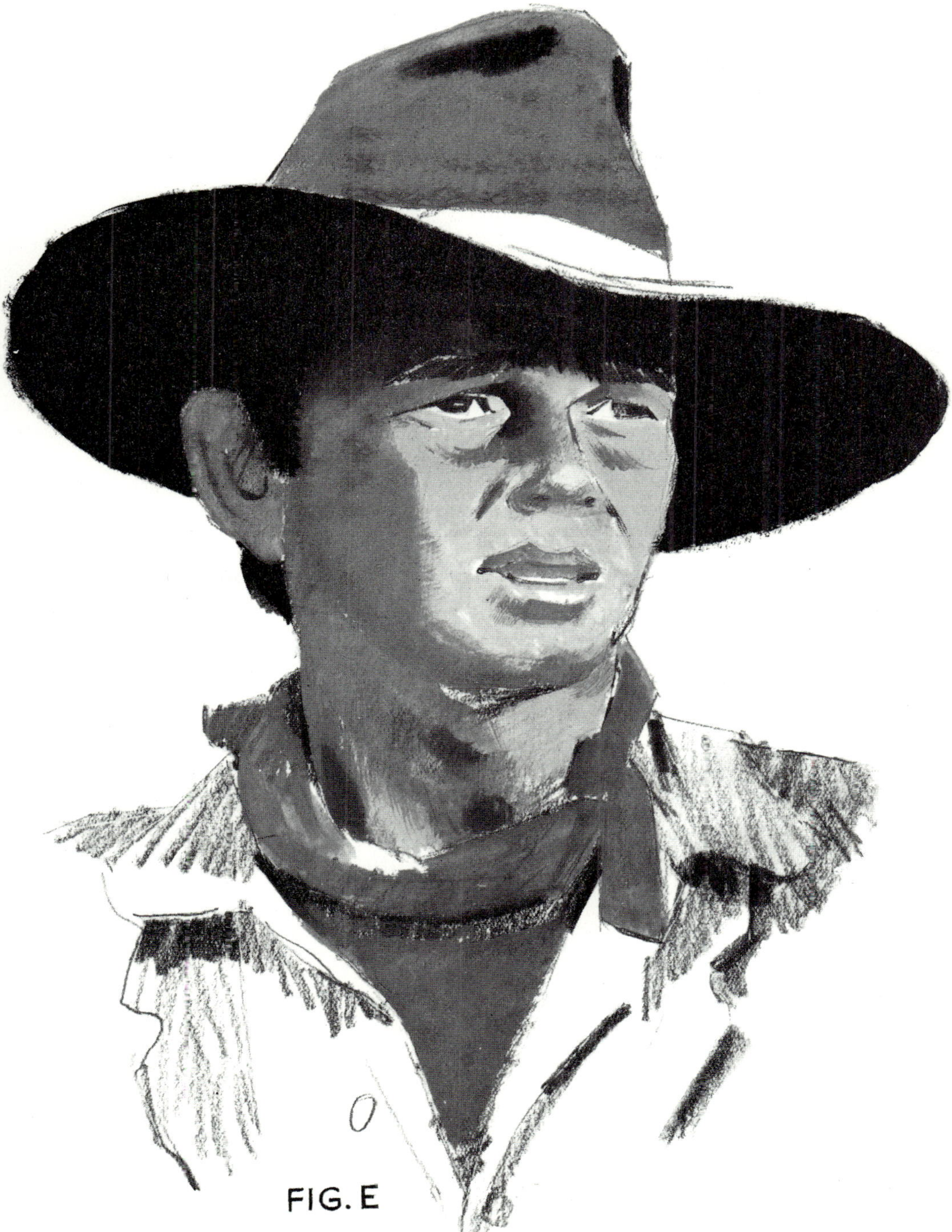

FIG. E

nose is achieved by dampening the previous graduation, painting with a very light grey, inserting this grey in the area between the eyebrows, graduating it and blending it with the central furrow and the lines on the forehead.

III. Eyes: These have to be painted and drawn really carefully. Try to note the different tones in the model and to apply them to enrich the expression of the glance. It isn't hard to paint eyes like these. Just work on them slowly and make an effort to make a good job of them. I left them, in the first place, almost finished and lacking only a touch or two, for example, to the crease of the lower eyelid, below the eyes themselves. These are wrinkles which you have to paint in the exact tone, neither lighter nor darker if you want them to be wrinkles and not just spots.

IV. The nose. I returned to this nose many times, mainly because of the shape of its lower part, the shadows made by the cheekbones at the side of the nose, and of the shape of the nostrils. As always, you have to make an exact copy, without adding anything out of your own head. The shapes and shadows of the model must be precisely copied.

V. The mouth: Take special care to paint exactly the black shown by the cavity. Note those spaces at the corners of the lips and extend that thin line between the rows of teeth. Make this black marking precise; you can do the rest relatively easily. You'll see that I haven't painted in the teeth or shown the space between one tooth and another, and that the top teeth are in shadow; a really very light grey is enough. Paint the lower lip with a little white of the former brightness and graduate it with the light grey of the remainder. With a tiny amount of water, moisten the limit of the upper lip where the moustache would be, and apply a little white, painting wet. Then graduate it to form the boundary of this upper lip. Lastly, graduate the shadow projected by the lower lip on to the top of the chin. I painted this graduation dry with my brush in the "comb" shape. This, however, came after the next section.

VI. The face: The result I had obtained up to this point in dealing with the chiaroscuro of the cheek and the rest of the non-shadowed part of the face did not fully satisfy me. In both the initial sketch and the later stage as in Fig. E, there was too much contrast between two tones — the shadow of the cheek remained harsh and did not correspond to the softness suggested by the model, so I

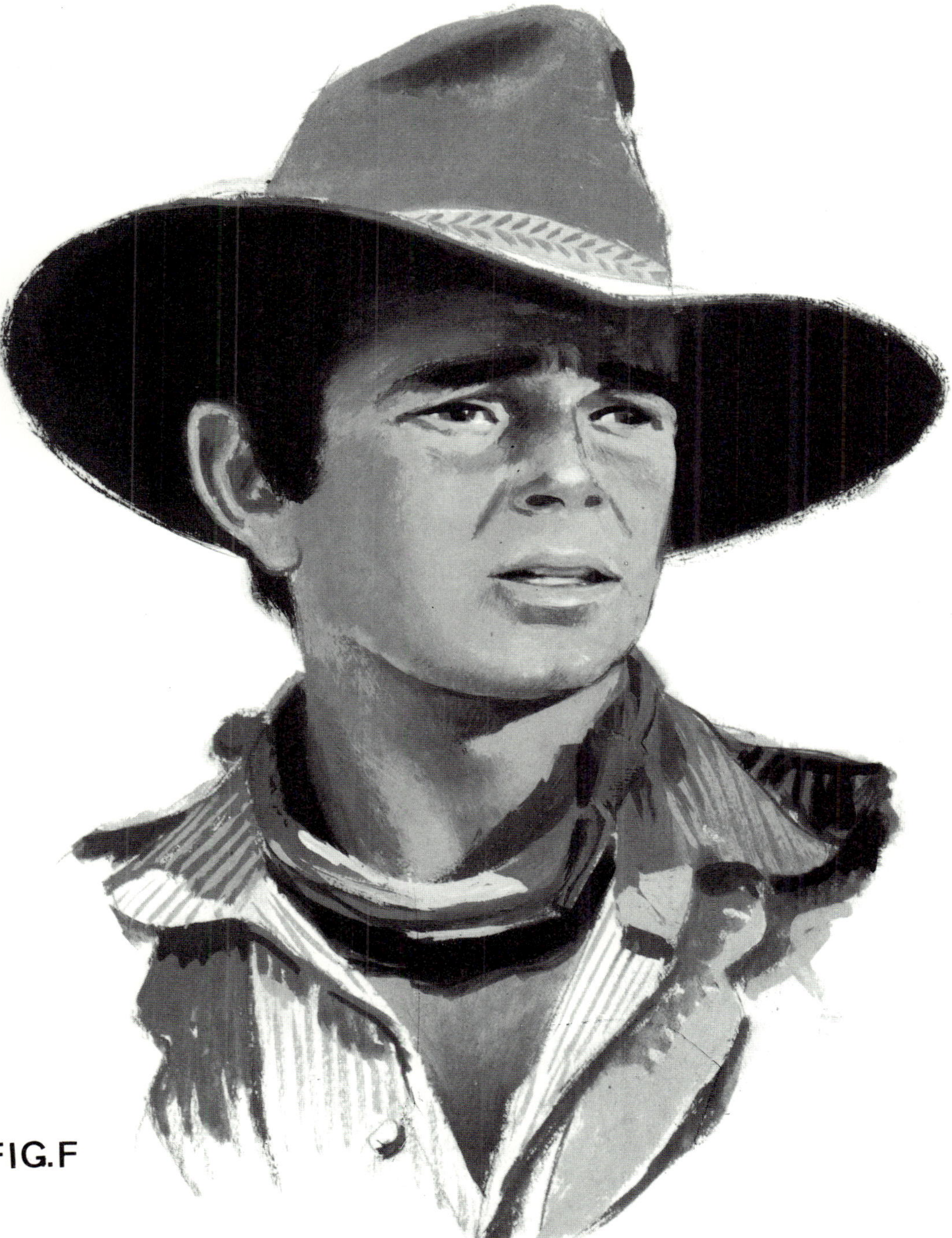

FIG. F

decided to tone down the shadow. This meant something like reconstructing the whole of the modelling of the face and repainting the graduations of the cheek, the tip of the chin and the nose. This was not entirely lost labour for me, however, because, owing to the general dampness of the whole of the face, I was able to strengthen the construction and the drawing of details such as the wrinkles on both sides of the nose and the slight shadow under the eyes, in the upper part of the cheeks. At the same time, I began with the grey of the cheek and the lighter grey of the face, and with the modelling of the neck.

VII. The neck: You have to work preferably moist, though some parts, like the main throat muscle, can be done dry. The same applies to the shadow projected by the chin and the one thrown by the handkerchief.

VIII. Hat: This must give the general feeling of having been painted freely. In the outline of the brim you'll notice a dry graduation — a slight toning down which gives the feeling of atmosphere. Don't forget this detail. The crease in the crown has been painted by dampening the whole thing. The dark vertical on the right, corresponding to the crease or fold of the other side, was achieved by a simple dry brush stroke.

IX. Chest or lower neck: A simple wet graduation, from bottom to top, but without joining up.

Free and more spontaneous treatment for the clothing

X. Handkerchief and clothing in general: It's best to become more free and easy here than with the rest of the picture, in order to enhance and emphasize the face. Note here the treatment given in Fig. F: in some places in the clothing the painting was done in a dark tone with a lighter tone applied over the top. This can be seen in the almost white highlights of the neckerchief, in the stripes of the neck of the shirt (in the shaded parts of that neck), in the point of the neckerchief which is draped over the lapel of the shirt, in the jacket lapel itself (left side), etc. This is done to give the work a greater pictorial quality, a greater tonal richness and greater freedom. Try it out and see for yourself.

And so, at last, there remain the ear, the border of the hair with the temple, the sideboards and the high-lit part of the nose. But none ot this is really very important for now. Once you've finished your first experiment with tempera, you can be quite pleased with your work.

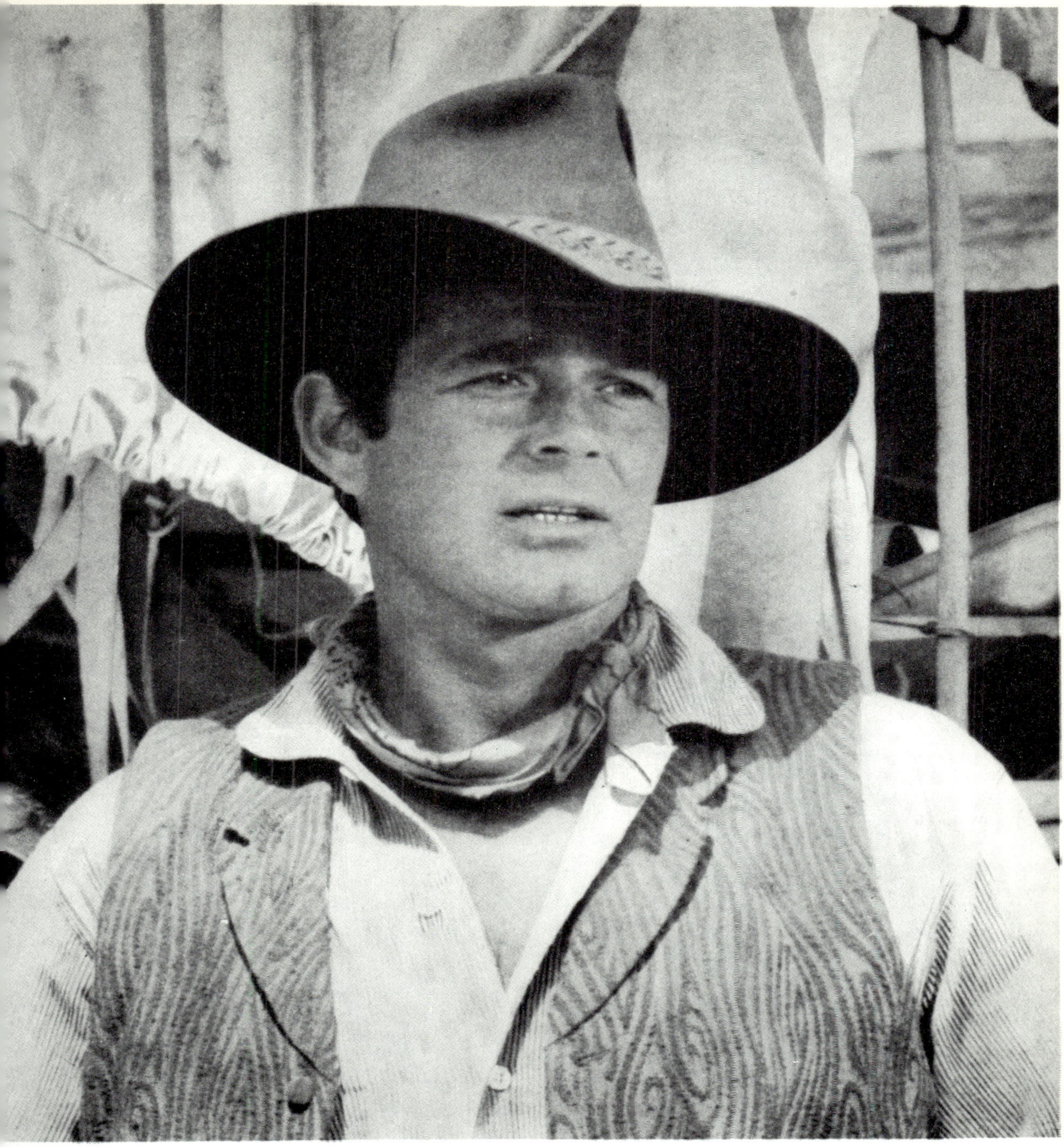

EXERCISE NO. 2 IN USING TEMPERA

BLACK AND WHITE PAINTING OF A STUDY FOR THE COVER OF A NOVEL. FIGURE OF A COWBOY FIRING A RIFLE

YOU WILL NEED THE SAME AS USED IN THE PREVIOUS EXERCISE, PLUS A 3B SOFT LEAD PENCIL.

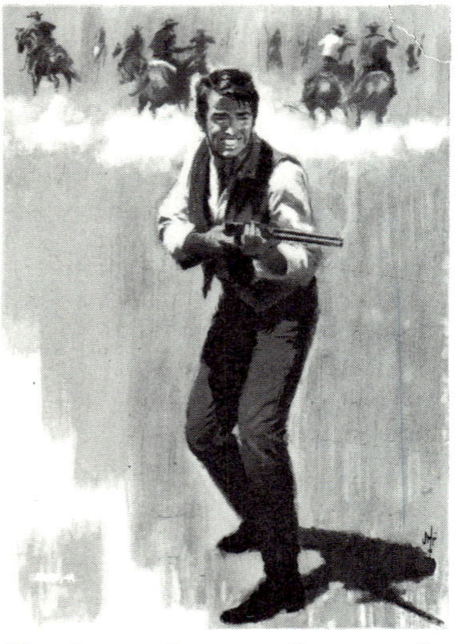

"In an effort to break the circle of Comanche Indians, O'Donnell orders his men to attack straight across the plain while he covers the retreat and keeps the remaining Redskins in check".

"This is the subject", the publisher says to you. "I'd like to have an exciting cover, something with a bit of bite to it. As you know, the novel's called "O'Donnell the Bold".

And off you go to your studio, and look up your reference library. There you find a photo from the film, *The Comanches* and start looking for ideas.

Paint a study in black and white tempera.

This is the exercise which we hope to see finished as a magnificent cover design painted in full colour.

HOW TO SET ABOUT IT

You will work from the photograph (a scene from the 20th Century Fox film *The Comanches*) in which you see one of the players holding a rifle. The figure of this cowboy with a few others, galloping along, with fighting in the background, will be your subject.

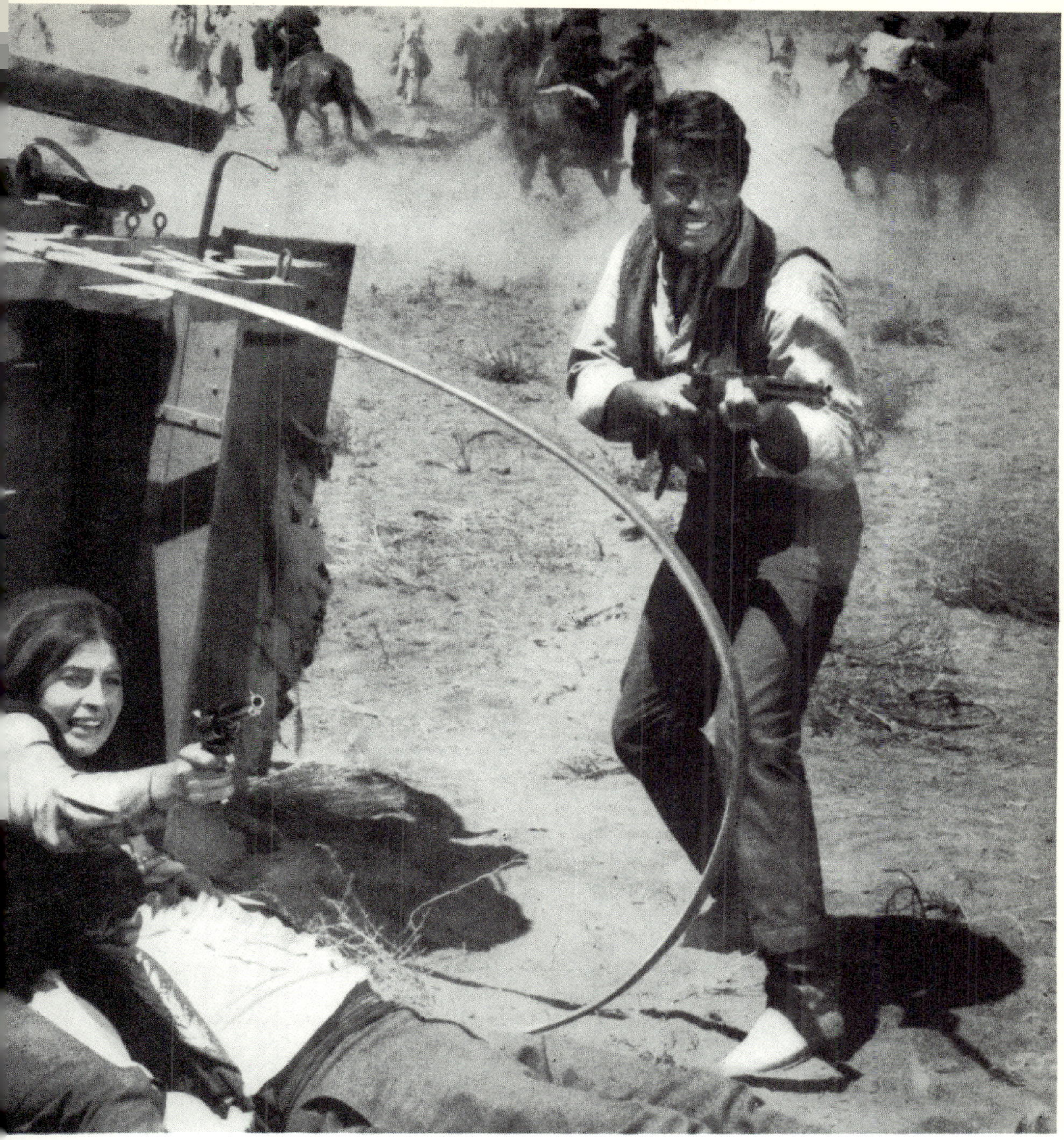

STAGE I: SQUARED-UP CONSTRUCTION AND TRANSFER

Begin by dividing up the photograph into squares, using a series of 1 cm squares which covers the figure in the foreground and the horsemen in the background. Draw this series of squares with a soft, sharp pencil or in Indian ink with a drawing-pen.

Square up the photo in 1 cm squares

Then repeat the same system of squares, increased to a size of 1.5 cm, and draw it with a soft pencil on ordinary thin paper: this gives you a figure which is bigger by half a size again. This is important.

Repeat the series of squares, increased to 1.5 cm on thin paper

The series of squares drawn over the photograph must measure 1 cm per square.
The series of squares drawn on the thin paper must measure 1.5 cm per square.

And so, the height of the figure in the photograph is 16 cm, while the figure you will draw will measure 24 cm.

Height of your figure: 24 cms

Fig. A shows my squared-up sketch.

Make sure the figure is well squared up, even marking out the limits of the passages from light to shadow, and ignoring the figures and everything else on the left-hand side of the photo.

See Fig. A

Now take a soft pencil, and 'paint' the back of the thin paper, transforming it into a kind of carbon paper; in other words, you trace the drawing.

"Paint" the back of the tracing paper

Transfer the drawing on to the final paper, tracing it on to a piece of good cartridge paper. Obviously you don't trace the squares!

Transfer the figure to the cartridge paper but don't transfer the squaring system

STAGE II: USING A SOFT PENCIL

Fig. B shows the state of the work at the end of this second stage which includes the work described below:

1. Reconstruction of the figure, drawing over the tracing, still working with a soft, sharp pencil.

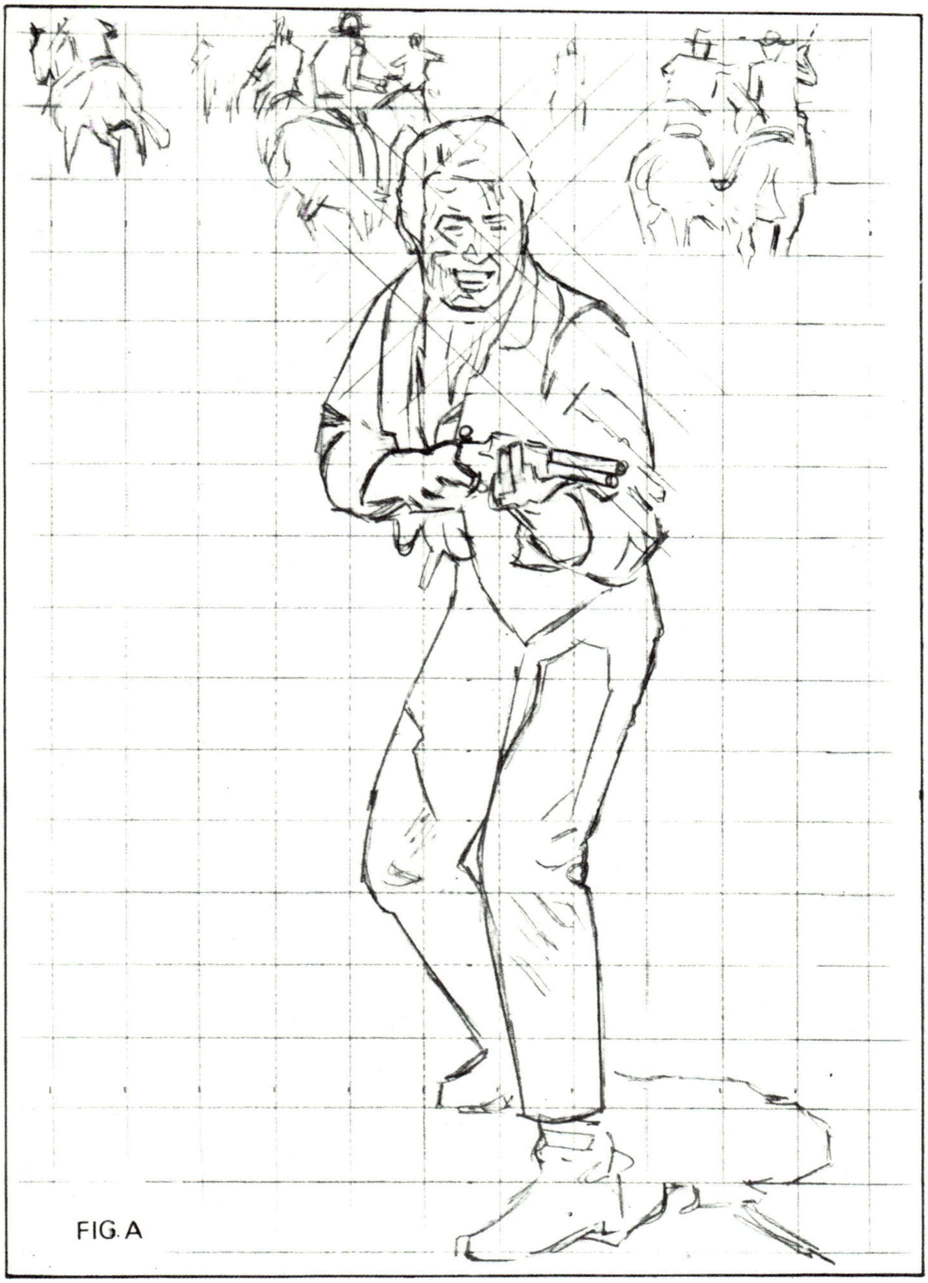

Slightly reduce the size of the head; make the body thinner; elongate the figure

So I slightly reduced the size of the head in relation to the body; made the body and legs thinner, and slightly elongated the whole figure (4 mm) in all, taking the measurement from the back foot and 6 mm measuring from the front foot.

2. Heightening the expressiveness in the figure, the lighting and slight modification of the final construction.

It's a good idea to stop here briefly and try to analyse which shapes, lights and shadows were affected by this interpretation. Look at Fig. B and the photograph while you are doing this.

As you know, the photograph of the man's body shows a flatter and bulkier figure. In order to achieve his effect, the illustrator has to stylize the figure by tapering and drawing out its shape.

Interpretation — with a few changes

On the question of essential alterations you'll note the lengthening of the rifle barrels and the shifting of them to the side. This way you get a less foreshortened view which brings the rifle more into prominence. The extended shadow which is cast on the ground by the figure provides a better relationship to the legs.

On the question of light and shade, you'll see a greater clarity in the reflected lights of the face, which enhances its size and expression; a greater intensity of tone in the neck of the shirt to emphasize the tones and planes of the face. There is also a greater selection of tones around the bottom of the waistcoat and the shadow of the trousers, below the model's left arm, and the progressive darkening of the front leg (ending in a boot which is almost black). In order to emphasize the height of the figure, set it off well and generally give it more vigour.

Enhance the values

As you can see in Fig. B, this stage revolves around the drawing and enhancing the values with the whole range of tones which a soft pencil supplies, filling in in black when needed.

STAGE III: TONING WITH TEMPERA

It's no good painting in a watered-down way, with tempera as liquid as though it were watercolour

Before you begin painting this exercise we have noticed that quite a few students following this exercise use mostly black watercolour and water and thus obtain a transparent finish, i.e., they paint in a watered-down style instead of tempera-style. This is no good. You really have to paint in tempera, getting your greys by mixing black watercolour with white tempera, thus achieving thick, covering tones. This is the only way to learn to work in this new medium, a medium which is of the greatest use when you remember

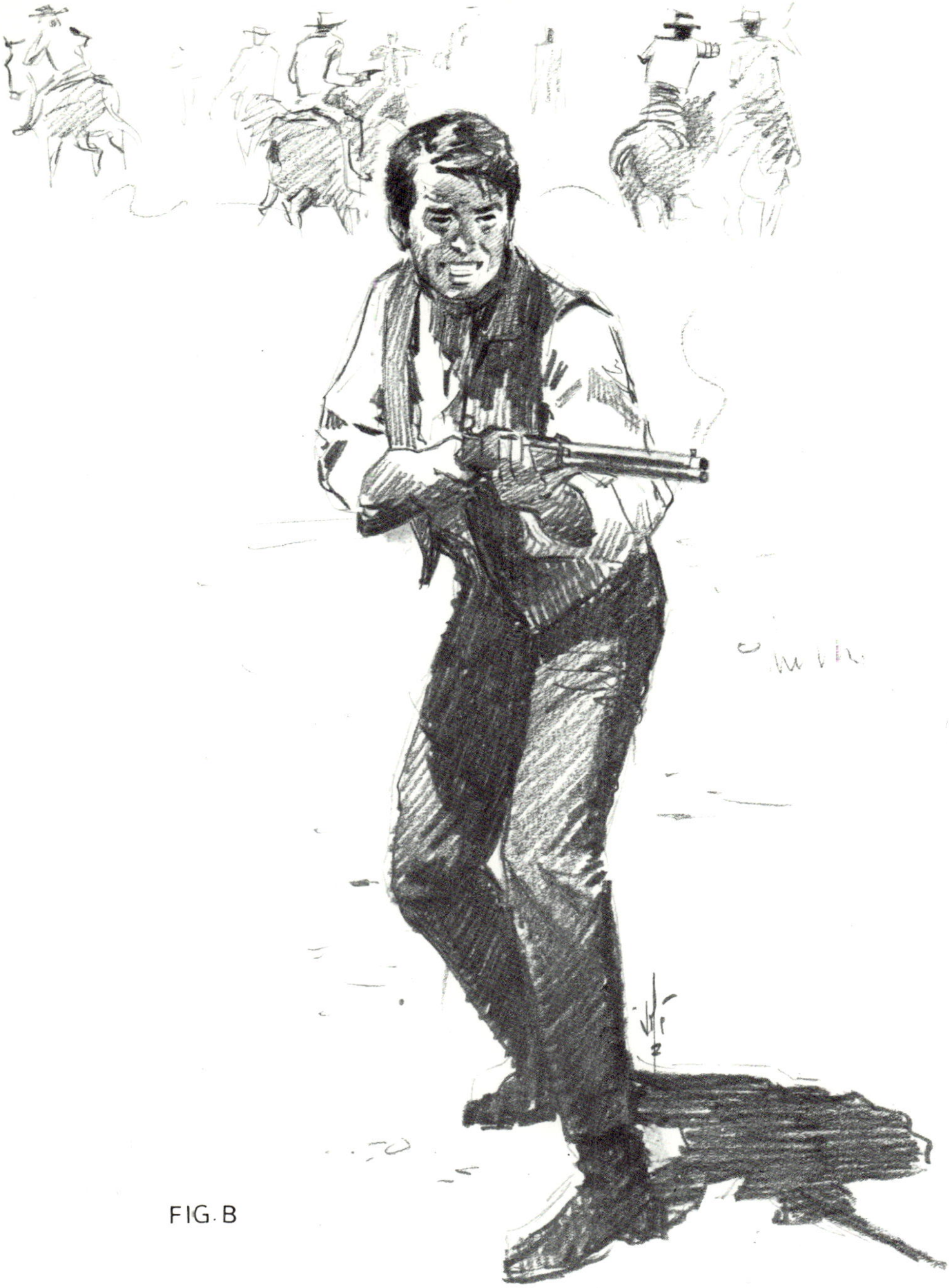

FIG. B

that tempera painting resembles painting in oils. You may feel it risky to lay the paint on thickly and cover the drawing. It won't be a matter of going all wrong, but merely of overcoming this difficulty, resembling the problems of oil painting.

Begin painting your illustration by compounding a very light grey, with which you'll paint the background later. Use a No. 10 sable brush, and try to achieve a more liquid mixture than usual — a colour which covers, but less of it.

Begin with the light grey of the background — Brush No. 10

It's a matter of painting by encroaching upon and partially covering almost everything which has been drawn: the horsemen in the background, the hair and face of the figure in the foreground, the shirt, arms, hands, etc, i.e., all the parts which need this grey to appear together with the brilliant whites and darker greys. (See Fig. C.) So paint away without any worries about going over the edges; just be careful not to lose the pencil guide-lines. The thing to remember is that you have to paint with a thick grey, but not thick enough to cover everything totally.

Paint this background by encroaching upon much of the figure, as though this did not exist

Finally, if you notice that, in some vital area, the grey is too opaque, dry the brush and absorb part of the colour. This will provide greater transparency.

Note in Fig. C, that the grey comes to an end when it reaches the lower left-hand corner; concentrate on an important point:

Stop the grey colouring when it reaches the corner. (See Fig. C.)

When you paint the background, brushstrokes must be vertical.

The purpose of cropping the background is to give more variety, apart from the possibility that the title of the work might take up that corner.

Painting with vertical brush-strokes provides a more artistic, more fluent or less affected result.

When this background colouring has dried, you'll have the feeling of painting on paper coloured light grey. Apart from preparing the ground so that you can paint with greater effect, this will supply you with the advantage of relying on a basic tone which has an effect on many parts of the picture as a half-tint in pellucid shadows and reflected light, etc.

Painting on grey paper

Begin by painting in some white, working with a very thick white, just as it comes out of the tube, so that it completely covers the previous grey. Paint in the white parts of the shirt and the most prominent highlights of the face. That should be satisfying.

Paint in some white parts with very thick paint

Now go ahead with some of the greys of the waistcoat and with the dark shadows of the trousers. Notice in Fig. C, that I have painted the shadow on the back trouser leg black.

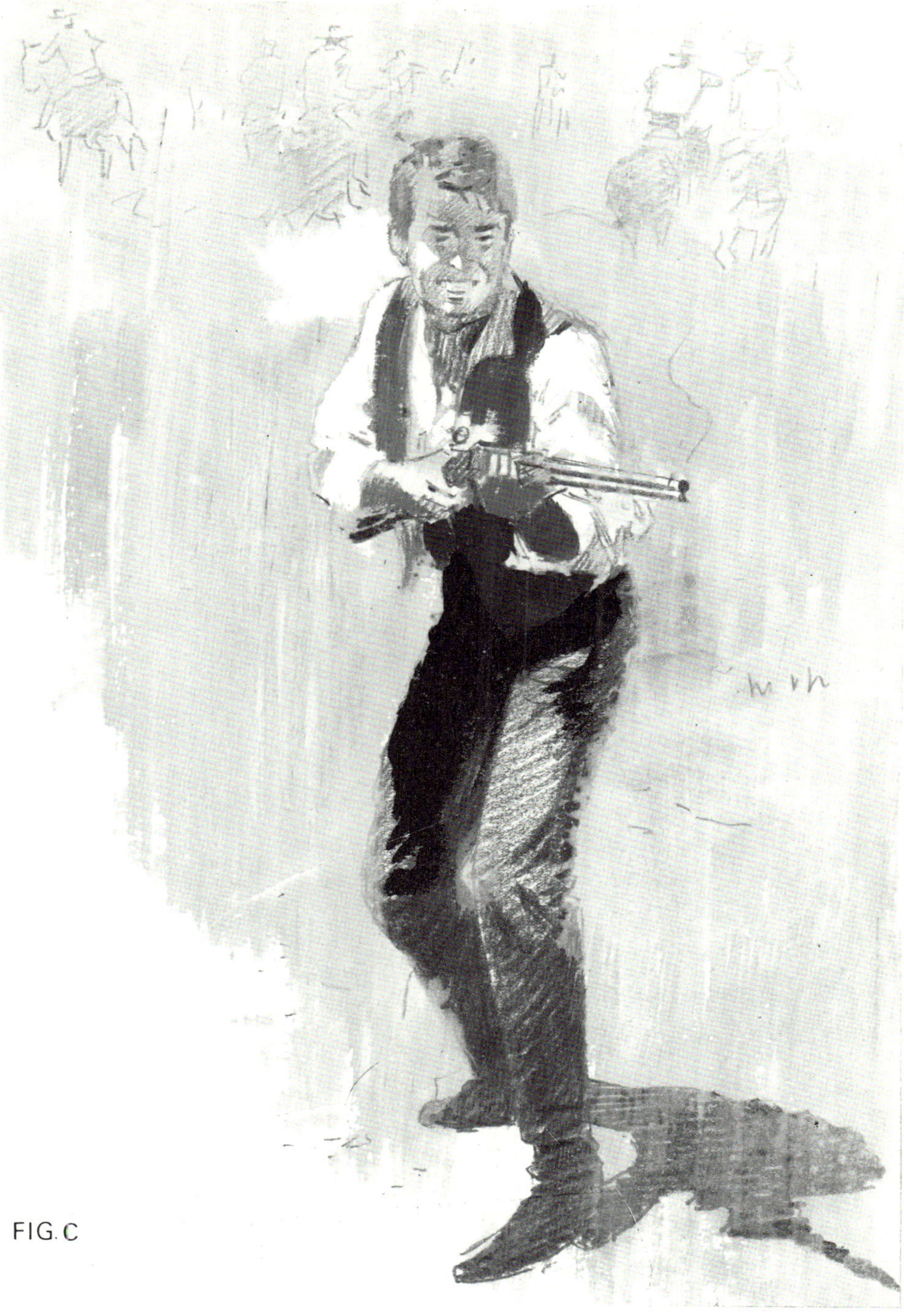

FIG. C

Going beyond this limit you can paint the light grey of this trouser leg, which corresponds to the highlighted part, above the black, and cover it all up as though shading in negative. This produces a more spontaneous and artistic result. The effect is the same as when you painted in the whites (over a grey background) of the shirt and the highlights of the face.

When you can, paint light over dark colours

In the photograph you can see that in the upper part, on a level with and behind the head of the central figure, there is a white area produced by the dust raised by the horses in the background.

These clouds of dust give a very effective impression, thanks, once more, to the grey background painted at the start. Fill your brush with white tempera, just as it comes out of the tube, and as thick as possible. Apply the paste over the area and then shade off the white with the tip of your forefinger or middle finger as though you were shading off the graphite of a lead pencil. This gives a good effect without much trouble.

Dust clouds painted with the finger

STAGE III CONTD. FINISHING TOUCHES

Fig. D, reproduced at the same size as your exercise, the original size, should explain what you should do to attain this final result. There are a few vital rules.

a. *You should almost always paint with a very thick colour, with practically no water, as though painting in oils.*

Very thick colour. Flat tints

b. *The bulk is achieved with flat tints or tones. In the majority of cases, the slight graduations existing have been achieved by painting dry, by hard rubbing, with the brush loaded with very thick colour.*

c. *This allows for a combined artistic result with dry application, while at the same time you attend to one part or another without any fixed order.*

Try to paint fluently, slightly at a distance, without too much attention to detail. Don't get stuck in one area; get on with it until you've finished. Go here and there, painting all over the place

Paint fluently and don't pay too much attention to detail

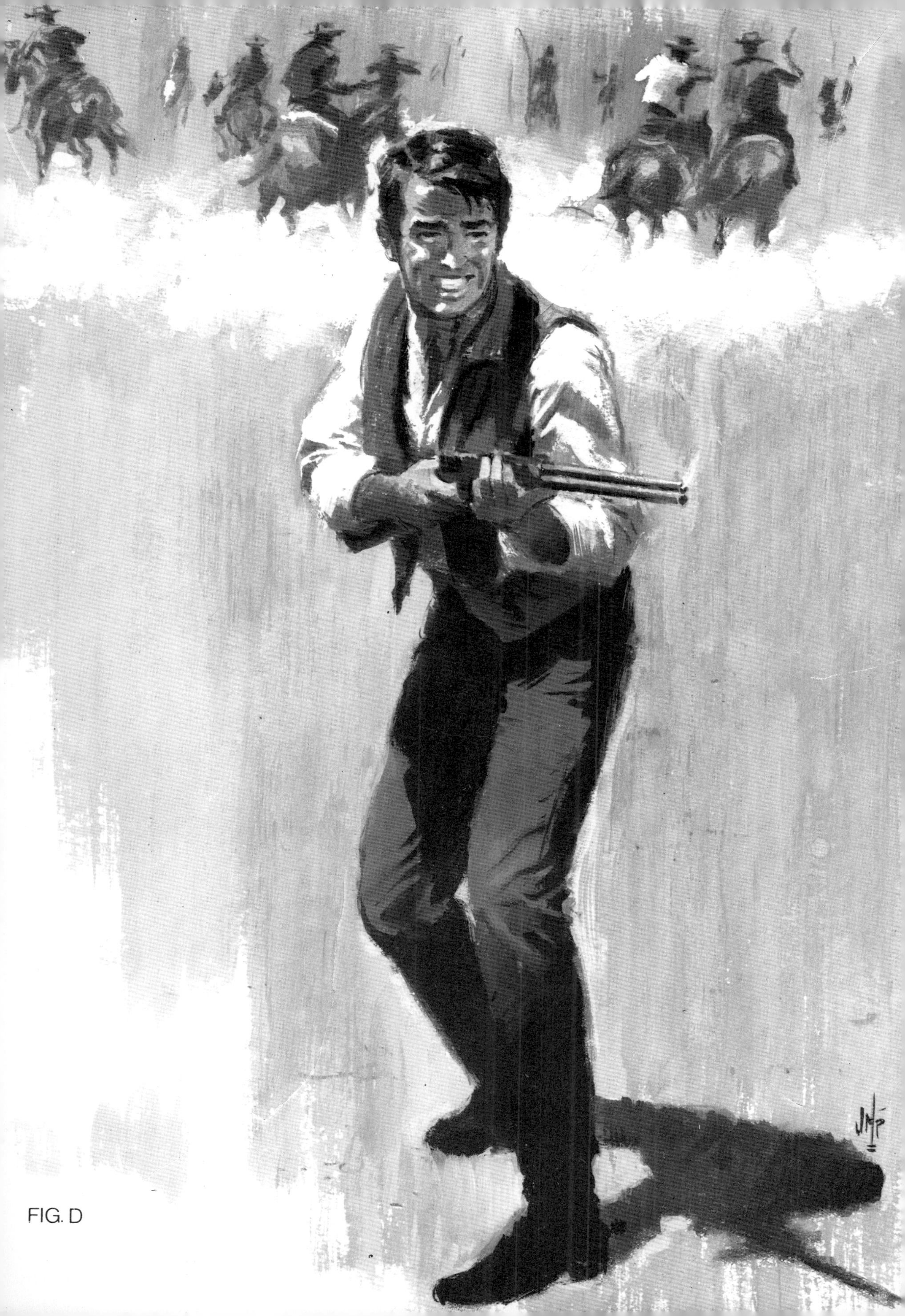

FIG. D

progressively, all at the same time. Whenever you can, paint in the negative, i.e., fixing limits and covering the darker tones with white or light colours. For example, that white which goes round the head, was painted when the hair was already finished, by covering again in white, and establishing the final outline. It's quite a difficult exercise, but very necessary — you're learning all the time.

MATERIALS USED FOR PAINTING IN GOUACHE OR TEMPERA

Tempera paint is usually obtainable in lead tubes and glass jars or bottles. It is important to keep the jars or tubes firmly sealed to prevent the paint from drying.

Sable brushes are most commonly used for painting in tempera. You'll need a minimum assortment, made up of Nos. 2, 4 and 6, as an essential for every kind of painting. The brushes reproduced here, in their original size and manufactured by the well-known brand, *Pelikan* correspond to the assortment mentioned.

Range of designers' gouache colours supplied by Winsor & Newton which provides an assortment comprisirig a total or nine colours to which white should be added.

(1) Brilliant Yellow, (2) Yellow Ochre, (3) Flame Red, (4) Madder Carmine, (5) Ultramarine, (6) Prussian Blue, (7) Viridian Lake, (8) Vandyke Brown, (9) Ivory Black.

EXERCISE USING GOUACHE OR TEMPERA IN COLOUR

SUBJECT: COVER OF A WILD WEST NOVEL

YOU WILL NEED: TEMPERA COLOURS, WATERCOLOUR PAINTS; BRUSHES NOS. 2, 6 AND 10; A SHEET OF CARTRIDGE PAPER; A RAG FOR DRYING BRUSHES; BASINS OR BOWLS FOR MIXING; WATER; SOFT PENCIL; INDIARUBBER.

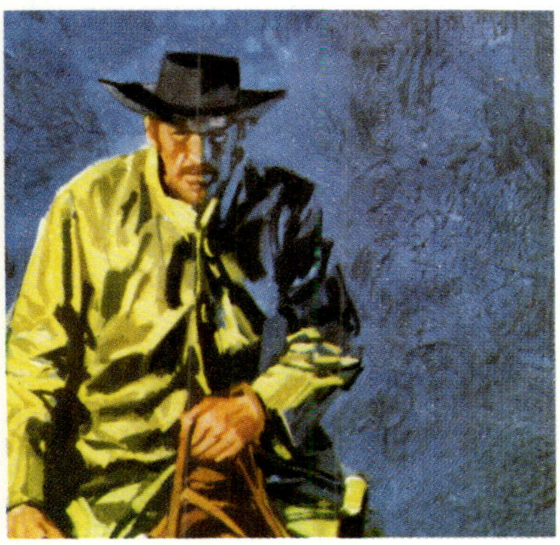

You have submitted the previous draft in black and white and the publisher tells you to go ahead, and to sort out the composition, position and size of the heading forming the title, the type of lettering and so on.

Lastly, as he hands you a note, he says:

"There's the title, the author's name and the logo.

All three things must appear, of course, with the name of the author being the smallest".

The height of the logo is about 2 cm at most. You can see it here. The original dimensions of the cover are 10.5 × 16 cm.

Your task is to paint the original for a front cover, finishing it off and working on the lettering, in the same way that it would be done if it were a job done for a publishing house.

Title of the novel:
O'DONNELL THE BOLD

Author: HARRY ROCKEY
Series: COWBOY

logo:

The medium to be used will be watercolour mixed with tempera (mainly white tempera). Other tempera colours play their part in painting large and non-abstract areas, or areas where spontaneity or energetic workmanship is needed.

STUDY OF THE COVER COMPOSITION ON A SEPARATE SHEET

When trying to study the composition of a front cover, the first step in professional work consists of making various advance sketches on a smaller scale than the original. You thus achieve your task more easily and at the same time you get a better view of the whole. So start by drawing a few rectangles on a separate piece of paper. They should be distinct from each other, and measuring 5.25 × 8 cm, exactly half the original size.

Initial measurement for previous studies: 5.25 × 8 cm

Now, drawing with a soft pencil, make a study on this scale of the cover composition. It's a matter of presenting the illustration, heading, author's name and series logo, each component being roughly sketched without detail but maintaining the proportions and tonal value of each component.

Draw your sketch with a soft pencil

As you try to make your composition, imagine what O'Donnell's real size could be in relation to the space available — is it a good idea to present the whole figure? What would happen if the figure were to be cropped above the knees, allowing the rest of it to be made larger? Or how would it be to create a proportionately smaller figure, leaving more space round it? All this is because the study carried out in the first sketch is aimed at analysing the potential of the photograph model. But so far there has been no attempt to solve the entire problem.

Aspects to bear in mind when making the composition

All the same, you have to think of a whole — an entire figure of this size — in proportion to the cover rectangle and so on. On the other hand, what would happen if the upper strip, including the horsemen, were to be placed lower down?

These questions are closely linked with the inclusion of the title, *O'Donnell the Bold.* This has to be considered in conjunction with the illustration: Where can I best place the title heading — which side should it go, how high should it be and how big should it be?

The heading

Finally, you have to decide upon the most suitable type of lettering. On the following pages you'll find six examples of types of lettering. Choose the one which you feel best illustrates the title, bearing in mind that the character of the lettering has to go hand-in-hand with the style and content of the illustration.

You must also decide whether the heading of the title should be in upper or lower case, on a single line or on two or more lines as follows:

Upper or lower case? One line or two

o'donnell, the bold

O'Donnell
the bold

O'Donnell
the
bold

O'Donnell **the** **bold**	**O'Donnell** **the** **bold**

Shown here are various suggestions for the composition of a title or heading intended for the front cover of a novel. They can be presented on one, two or three lines. These examples combine upper and lower case letters and are ranged right or left. More types of lettering are shown on the next two pages.

A B C D E F G H I J K L M N O
P Q R S T U V W X Y Z
1 2 3 4 5 6 7 8 9 0
a b c d e f g h i j k l m n o p q r
s t u v w x y z

Grotesque New Haas.

A B C D E F G H I J K L M
N O P Q R S T U V W X Y Z
a b c d e f g h i j k l m
n o p q r s t u v w x y z

Super Black Folio.

ABCDEFGHIJKLM
NOPQRSTUVWXYZ
abcdefghijklmno
pqrstuvwxyz

Clarendon.

A B C D E F G H I J K L M
N O P Q R S T U V W X Y Z
abcdefghijklmnopqr
sutvwxyz

Mannequin.

A B C D E F G H I J K L M
N O P Q R S T U V W X Y Z
a b c d e f g h i j k l m
n o p q r s t u v w x y z

A B C D E F G H I J K L M
N O P Q R S T U V W X Y Z

Italian.

The professional will plan three or four samples until a pair of acceptable sketches are chosen.

In the three pictures below, you'll see I have supplied three possible ideas concerning this cover composition. In the first, the cowboy is moved slightly to the right so that the heading, ranged left, can take up more space. In the second, the figure moves into the centre, and the title is also centred, at the bottom. The lettering is reversed (white against the coloured background) and is superimposed on the cowboy's legs. This calls for a very colourful background in order to create the contrast necessary to make the lettering stand out and be legible. In the third composition the figure is shown cropped at knee-level, making it more of a close-up. The reversed lettering below is superimposed on the figure and the background.

In these three examples, the composition of the heading is two-line, with "O'Donnell" standing out on the first line, and "the Bold" in smaller lettering on the second line. The characters are fairly large, forming a compact patch, each offering a distinctive type of lettering which should be considered on the basis of legibility, and suitability to the theme.

HOW TO PAINT IN WATERCOLOUR AND WHITE TEMPERA

The mixing of a watercolour paint with white tempera supplies

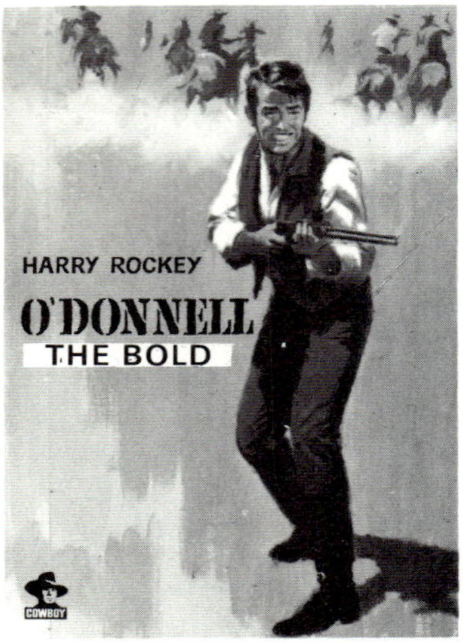

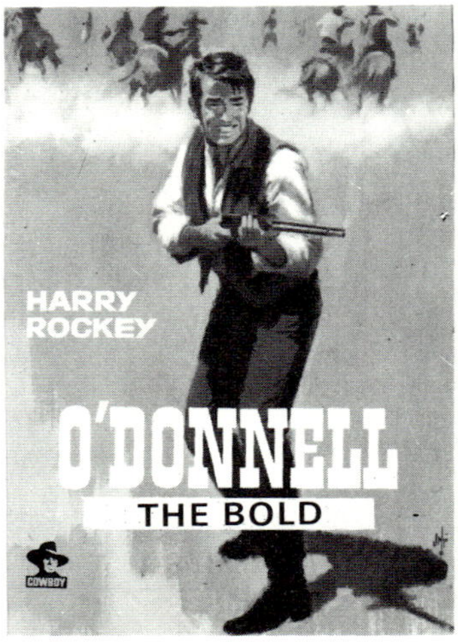

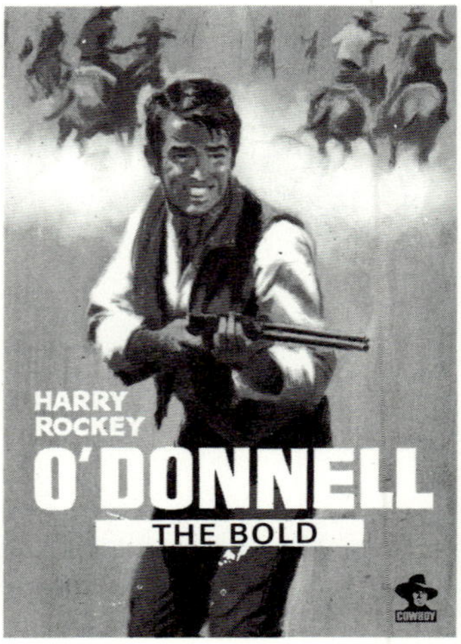

an opaque, covering colour, which means you can paint light colours over darker ones. Let's experiment:

To test, mix white tempera with watercolour

I. Begin by loading your No. 10 brush with the most intense colour of your box of watercolours — carmine, for example. Dilute this colour in the same mixing palette with very little water to achieve a thick, concealing paste. Then paint a uniform patch on a piece of drawing paper.

II. Wash the brush out thoroughly with plenty of water, remove most of the water and, with a very little water, load it with white tempera till the brush is thoroughly soaked and you obtain a thick paste.

III. By now the carmine patch will not be completely dry. Mix the white tempera with the carmine watercolour and paint a graduation from dark carmine to white, passing through magenta, pink, etc.

IV. Now wait until the graduation is completely dry. In the meantime wash the brush again, take on a little ochre watercolour, mix it with white tempera to achieve a cream colour and...

V. When the carmine is dry, paint over it with this cream. Then try a medium green made up of watercolour green and white tempera. You'll find it looks good.

Why some professionals paint in tempera and watercolour

The quality with which you have been experimenting, combined with the brilliance of colouring suplied by the watercolours and the fact that you are able to paint at times with watercolour alone is a great advantage. It gives a transparency to the painting and helps you with the difficult bit. Some professional artists prefer the mixture of both media.

Thick paint in some parts, transparently in others

So in this exercise, ifs a matter of painting with the technique of tempera, using thick watercolour or rather, watercolour and thick tempera, developing the technique of watercolour painting in some sections and then painting transparently, using the white of the paper.

Tempera in large sections

Watercolours for small and carefully constructed areas

Where do you have to use one technique and where the other? Tempera should be used in the larger parts which need ease and spontaneity, such as backgrounds and clothing. Watercolour will be more suitable for painting small areas where the construction needs more care, such as faces and hands.

This does not mean that in these watercolour areas (faces and hands), the artist cannot apply a few strokes of tempera or thick, concealing paint to create highlights and brilliant patches, certain reflections in shadows and so on, in order to achieve a move vigorous style in harmony with the rest of the work.

Painting the "O'Donnell" cover

Background: The first layer should not be too thick; it should be half-concealing, but with plenty of colour. This layer can go over the figure, but the face and the hands should remain untouched.

Later, when the painting is almost completed, you may emphasize this background with thicker paint.

Face: Paint this first in watercolour alone with no white tempera, obtaining the whites through transparency. When you have achieved a good colouring and a perfect play of light and shade, try to improve on it, creating contrasts and enhancing it with a few touches of watercolour mixed with white tempera. This can be very effective for the highlights and brilliant patches of the cheeks, nose and illuminated side of the face.

Face: in watercolour, with touches of tempera

Hair: Paint with tempera.

Hair: tempera

Clothing: You can paint it in general using thick tempera. But it's safer to begin with a thinner mixture — you'll still have the chance later on to emphasize with thicker paint.

Clothing: tempera

Hands: With watercolours initially, later retouching in tempera.

Hands: watercolour

Horsemen in the background: Initially in watercolours, but painted over again in tempera.
By now, you must be wondering about colour.

Horsemen: first in watercolour: then in tempera

COLOURING AT LAST

We have been able to give you here a series of reproductions* in colour for the cover of "O'Donnell", and have invited you to follow the process and to paint with the same colours. In this exercise you can choose, compose and apply the colours, experimenting for yourself and creating the colours by yourself, as the professional does.

To help you in this task, we are reproducing three examples of front covers painted by Jorge Longarón, and published by Toray.

Front covers already published, as colour references

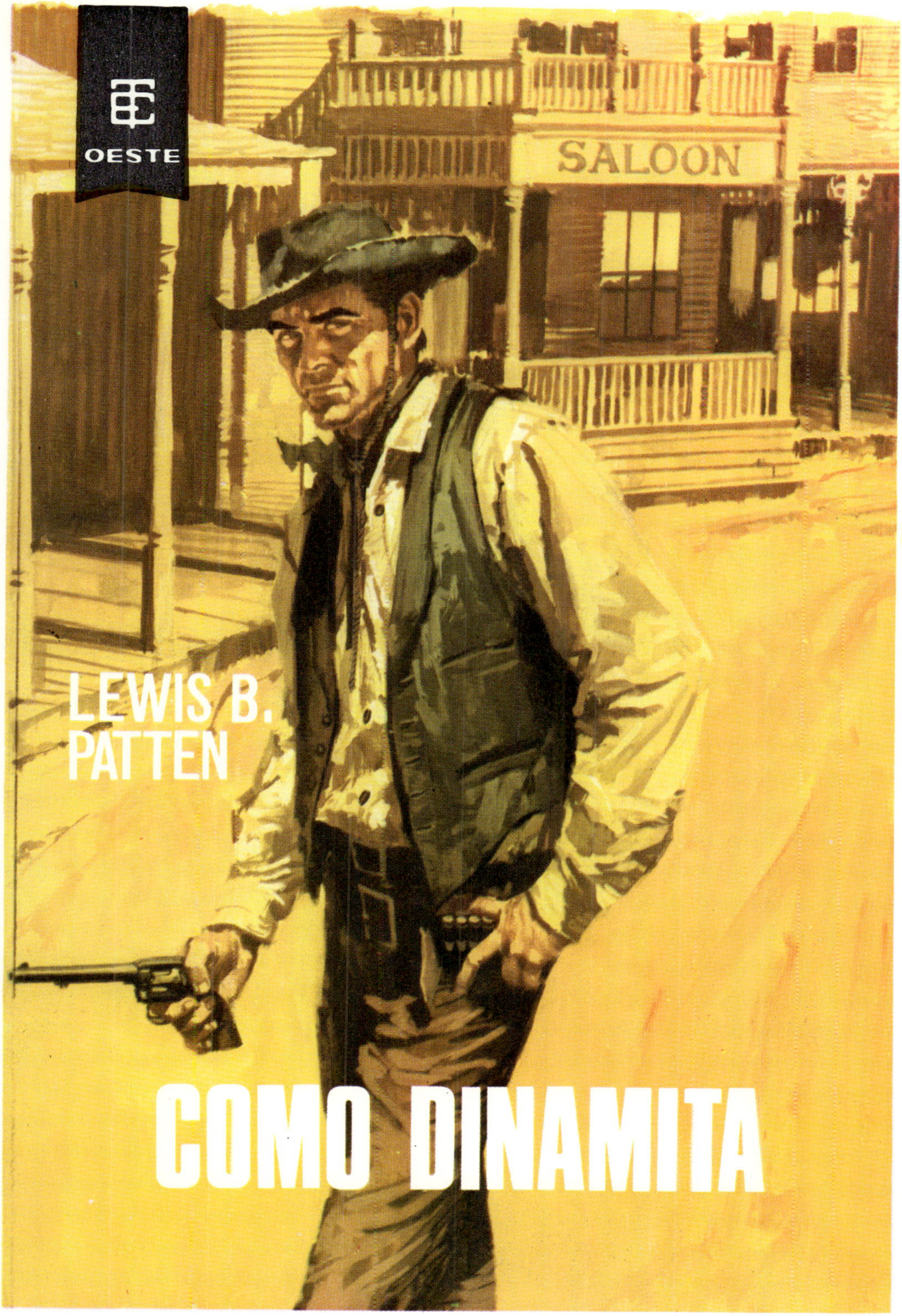
OESTE
SALOON
LEWIS B.
PATTEN
COMO DINAMITA

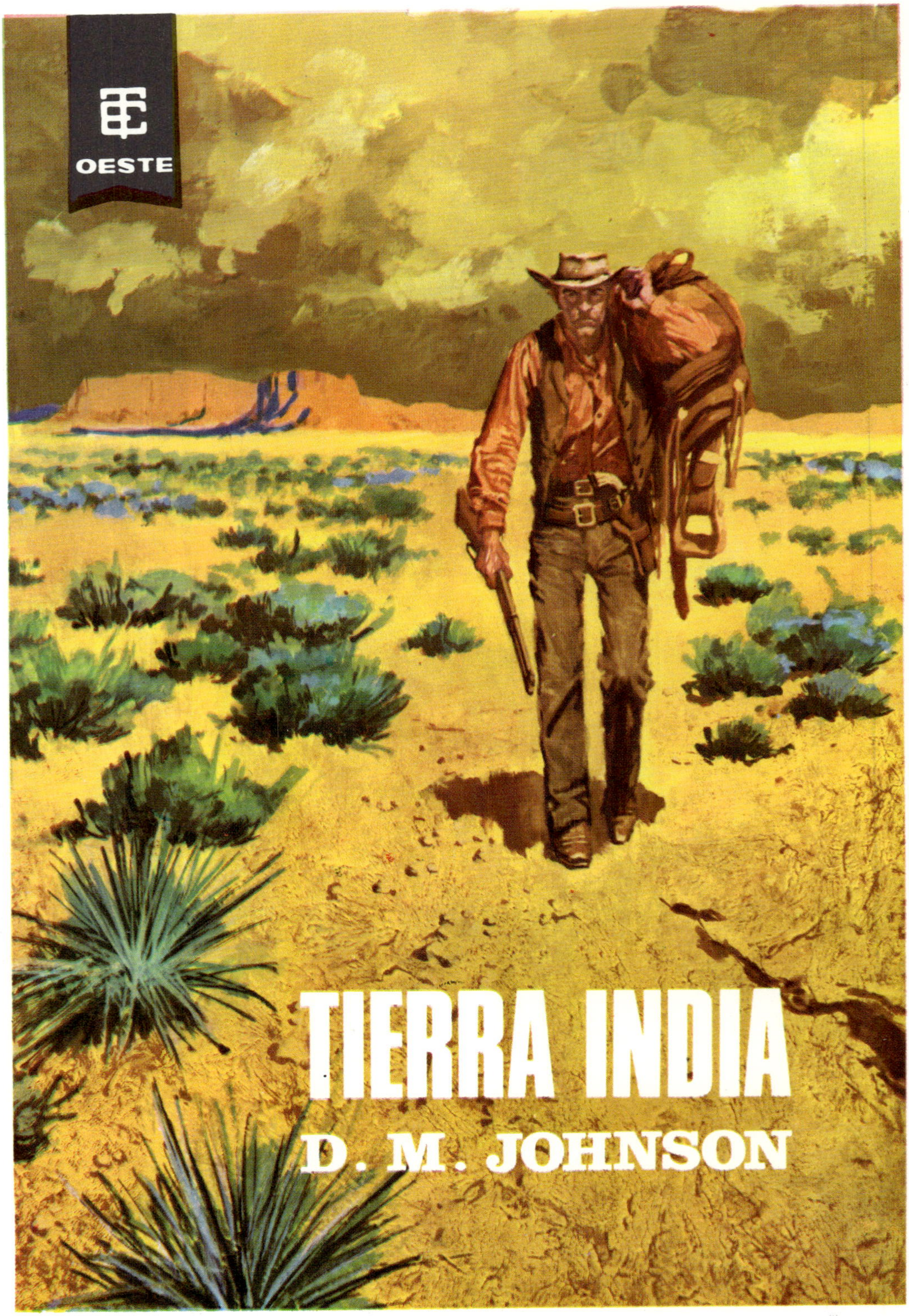
ŒC
OESTE
TIERRA INDIA
D. M. JOHNSON

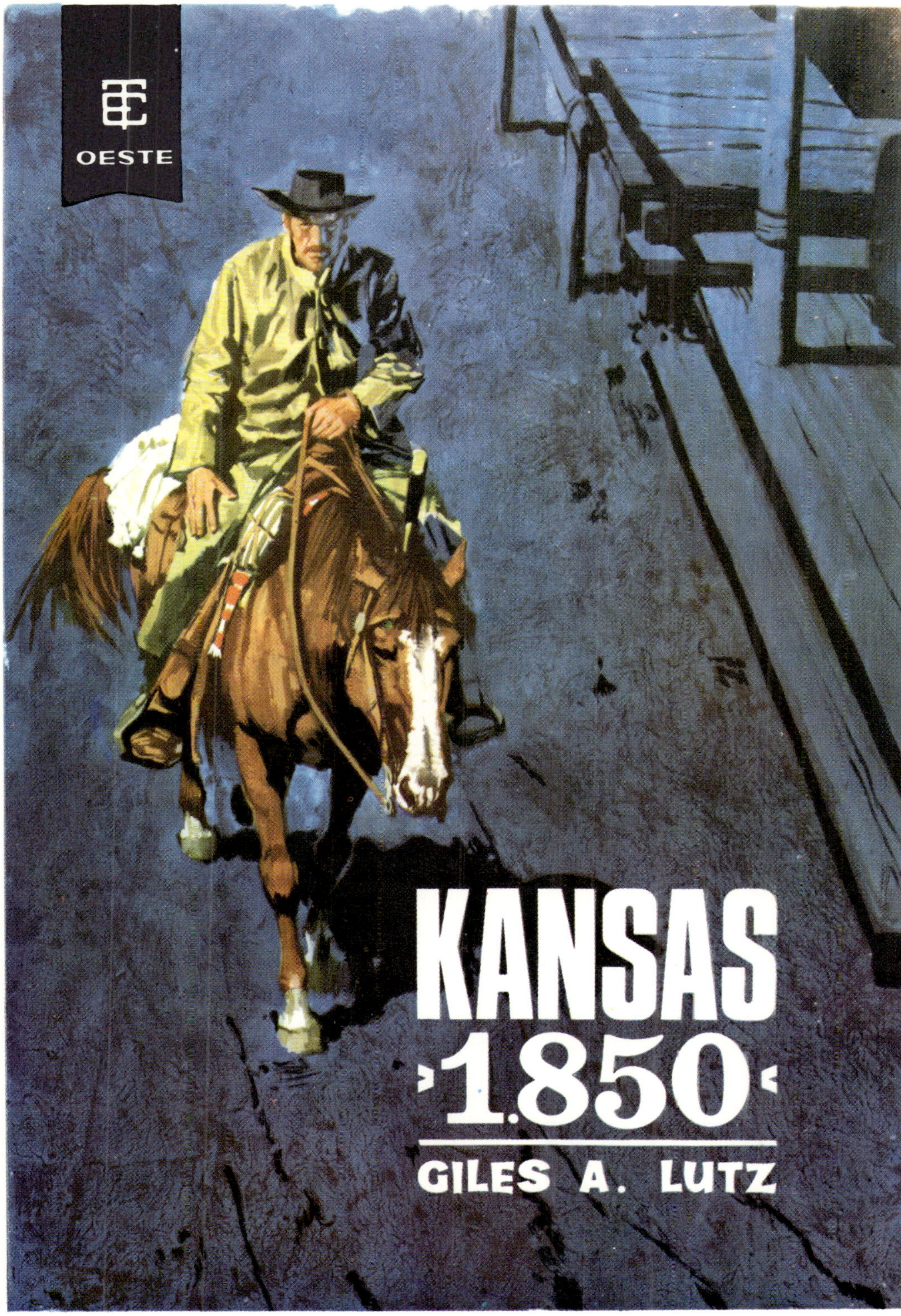
OESTE
KANSAS
1.850
GILES A. LUTZ

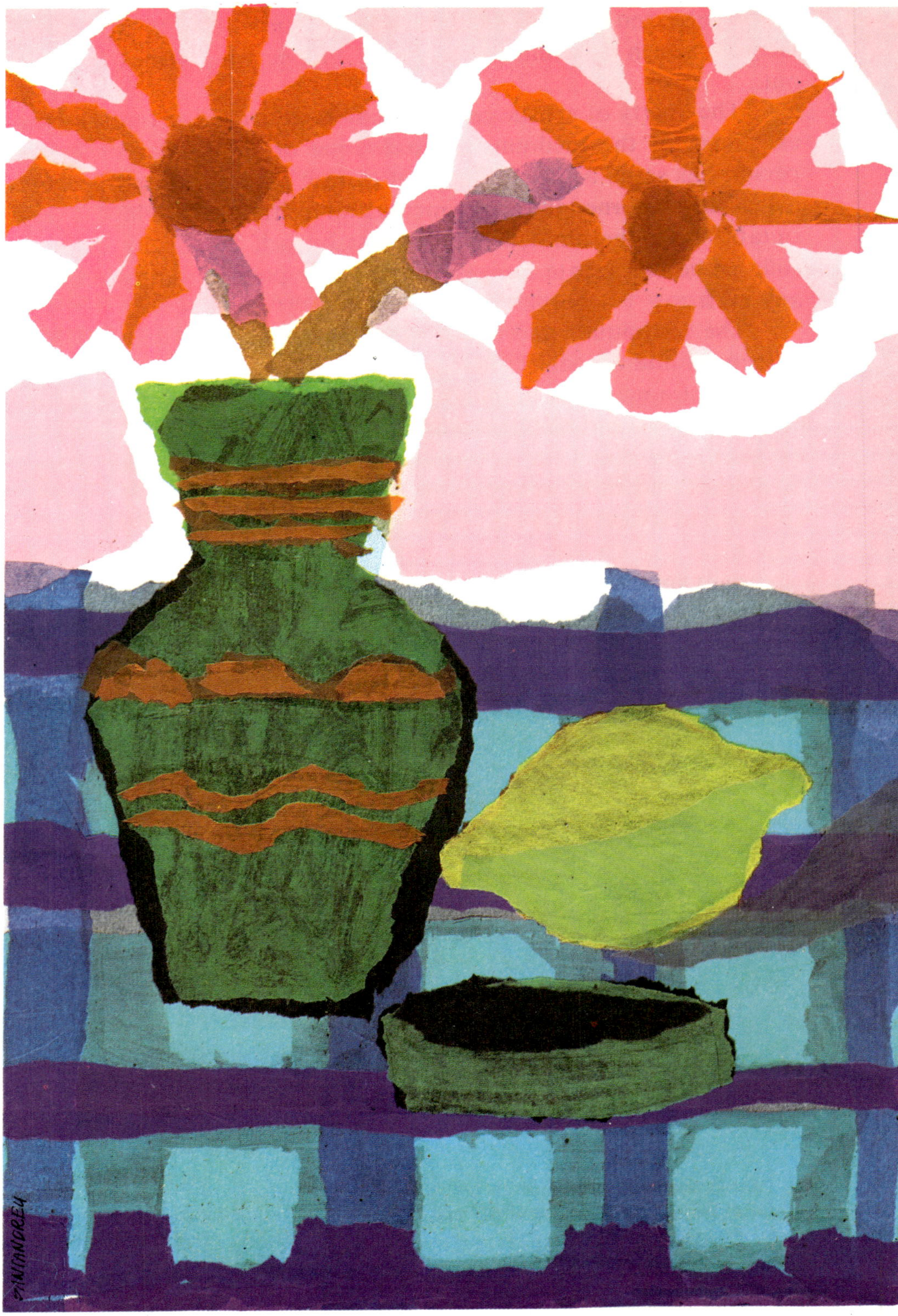

HOW TO CREATE A COLLAGE

There's no true technique for collage; in collage there is no drawing or painting which might be compared with techniques such as pastel, watercolours and oils.

Collage has no technique

Collage has no technique, but it requires craft, i.e., a practical knowledge of the materials which occur in collage and the potential which they afford. Here is a study of these materials.

MATERIALS COMMONLY USED IN COLLAGE

Backing used in collage

BACKING: In general, rigid, thick supports are needed to make it simpler to stick on each component. As we will shortly see, these elements may be thin, thick, light or heavy; therefore it's advisable to have a backing made of cardboard or wood prepared with a coat of distemper or lined with cartridge paper, either white or coloured. For small works in collage, thick Bristol-board is advised.

Adhesives

GUM OR GLUE: You can use an ordinary adhesive such as paste, rubber solution, gum arabic or glue from a tube, etc., for gluing on lightweight materials such as bits of paper, a piece of fine cloth, photographs, etc. And you'll need thicker gum, such as carpenter's glue, cement paste, plastic gum, etc., for fastening solid and heavy bodies, such as cardboard, sand, crushed or sanded glass, bits of thick cloth, buttons, small pieces of metal, etc.

Papers and Bristol-boards

THIN AND NORMAL PAPER AND BRISTOL-BOARDS: I refer to coloured papers and Bristol-boards, especially tissue paper; and cellophane in the way of thin papers; and as ordinary papers especially varnished paper, glossy paper and wrapping paper; for thick paper I mean Bristol-boards, glossy paper in general, linen and tooled paper, i.e., those which have a small pattern in relief.

Splendid works can be achieved with the exclusive use of coloured paper. You tear up tissue paper and create shapes and colours by superimposing them, as did the artist, Juan Santandreu, for example, whose collage is reproduced opposite.

Collage with tissue paper

In this case, Santandreu makes use of the effects of transparency by using thin tissue paper. And with the help of coloured varnished paper, other effects can be achieved through their opacity. It is also as well to think about the combination of transparent papers, such as cellophane, and opaque papers, such as varnished paper, or about the effects supplied by crimped Bristol-boards which give the impression of texture.

Collage with printed pieces of advertisements

PHOTOGRAPHS AND PRINTED PAPER CUTTINGS: In this section we include all kinds of photographs, black and white and coloured and also any other class of printed paper, from pieces of ordinary newspaper with headlines and texts, to the many-coloured fragment of an illustration or image. In general, these components take their place in a collage as fragments or parts of a whole. It is possible, however, to construct a magnificent collage using only pieces of colour-printed paper. Use them like this: a composition is devised on a white or grey Bristol-board. This is sketched in pencil. Then various advertisements or illustrations from colour magazines are selected and cut out. In the shapes and colours of these printed pages an attempt is made to consider the colouring and shapes making up the already sketched picture. Lastly, pieces from the coloured pages are cut out and stuck on, and the shapes are used for "painting" and constructing the shapes and colours of the picture or subject proposed.

Varied materials

VARIED MATERIALS: The most varied materials are used here; these are governed only by their suitability for the plan for which they are intended. The list is a vast one: sackcloth, leaves from trees, cog-wheels from watches, wood shavings, flakes of cork, plastic, sawdust, etc.

Methods for cutting

SCISSORS AND "FINGERS" FOR CUTTING: We say, "Fingers", taking the place of scissors, because there are many types of collage (like the one we mentioned by Santandreu or the one we shall see later by Plá Narbona) in which the paper, cuttings or light cardboard are torn with the fingers to get certain shapes.

TWO SYSTEMS FOR MAKING A COLLAGE

Putting glue on the component or on the backing

Either stick your materials on by gluing the component, or stick them on by putting glue on the backing. When the components are thin, e.g. paper, cuttings or light cardboard, the best thing to do is to put the glue on them and apply them direct. When the material is thick (cardboard, cork, textiles, etc.), or is in the form of particles (sand, sawdust, small bits of glass, etc.) the best thing to do is to cover the backing with a thick coat of glue, leave it to dry until it adheres well and place on it whatever material may be required, or scatter on the sawdust, sand, crushed glass, etc. The results, of course, are each unique.

FROM THEORY TO PRACTICE

Make collages from paper with varnished, matt and black surfaces.

YOU WILL NEED: VARNISHED, MATT AND BLACK PAPER OR ELSE THIN, BLACK MATT PAPER; LIGHT WHITE CARDBOARD; SCISSORS; INSTANT GLUE; TWO PIECES OF GLASS THE SAME SIZE AS THE COLLAGE.

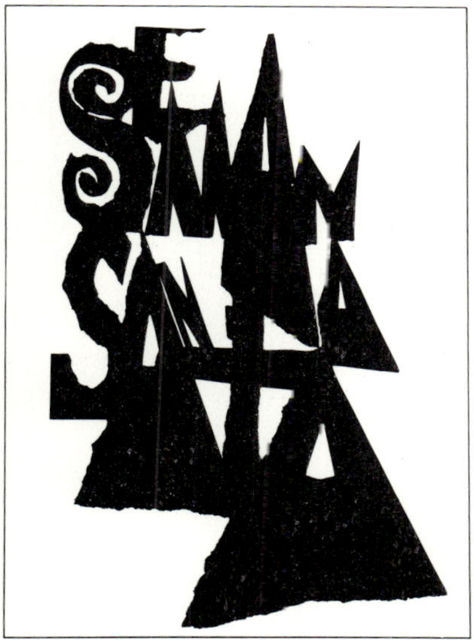

José Plá Narbona has created a magnificent series of illustrations for a book of poetry; some were published as outstanding examples of creative art in books and magazines on art. Narbona used only the process of sticking pieces of black paper on a white background.

With a few simple pieces of black paper on a white background making up two words: *Semana Santa* (Holy Week), he recently created a remarkable poster with which he won, in world-wide competition, the first prize for posters in the International Exhibition for Applied Arts, Punta del Este, Uruguay. This prize set the whole

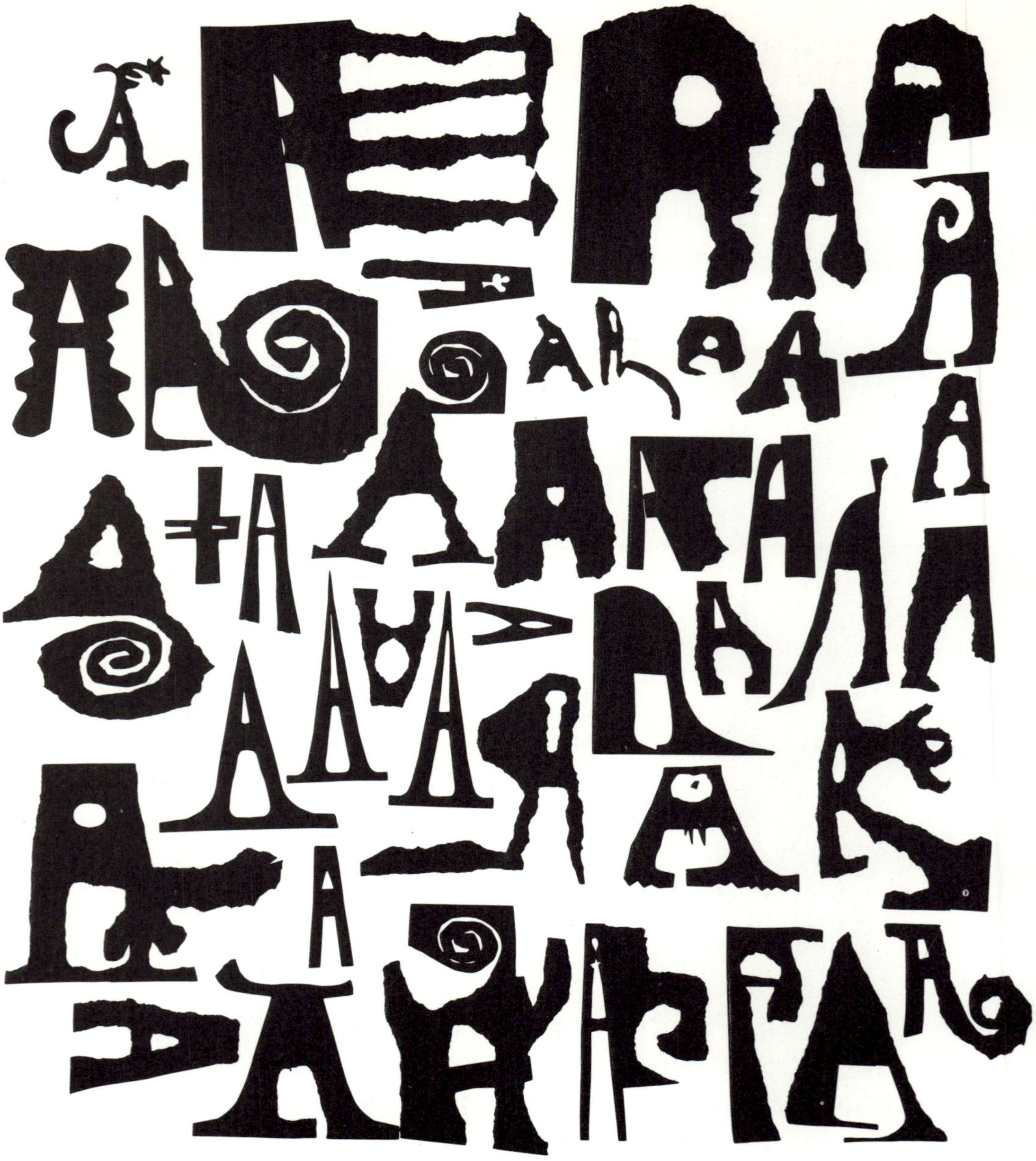

Spanish press talking because of its importance and because it was won by a Spaniard the first time it was put up for competition.

In the following pages, Plá Narbona explains how he treats this form of collage.

Plá Narbona explains that this type of collage is more tricky than it may seem. You need a deep knowledge of drawing and composition together with the true artist's curiosity. Otherwise it's impossible. There are no short cuts. In order to achieve this apparent

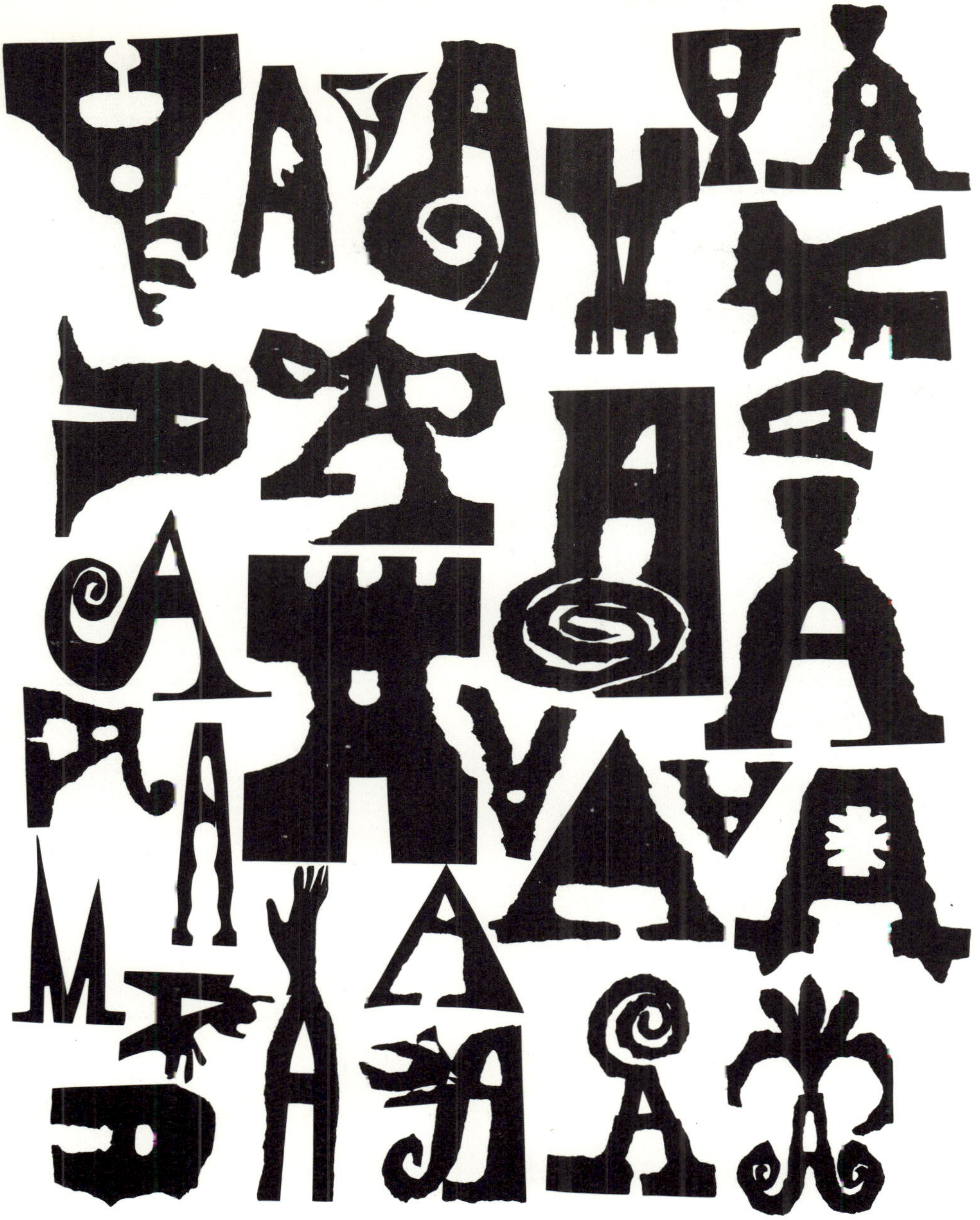

simplicity, this synthesis of the picture, you have to cut, pare off and tear up tiny but real mountains of black paper. Narbona says: "To achieve this Holy Week poster I spent many hours constructing letters: Ss of every kind, form and size, torn out by hand or cut with scissors, or by both methods at once. I made dozens of Ms and As, too. I remember I was making a letter (I ended up by making all the letters of the alphabet to make names with)! and I cut it and tore it, looked at it for a few moments on white paper and placed it at once among the "good" or "fair", or I threw it on the floor, along with the "bad" ones. I remember once I was using a piece of the card measuring 24 × 30 cm. I was experimenting and trying to compose a collage with the title *Holy Week*. And I remember that I went on working like that for three afternoons and a morning, and that due partly to luck and largely to the great amount of material selected, little by little, the poster took shape".

Final process in which photography plays a part

Plá Narbona, besides being an excellent draftsman, painter and engraver, is also an exceptional photographer. He has a large photographic laboratory with all he needs. Plá Narbona and his assistants, besides using photographs for illustrating the covers of books, magazines, catalogues, etc., also work at his illustrations, drawings and paintings. Once he has summed up the scene and decided where everything can go, he puts a few drops of glue on the pieces of black paper, sticks them on the background and then places the cuttings between two sheets of glass so that the top piece presses upon and evens out the strips of black paper. The sandwich

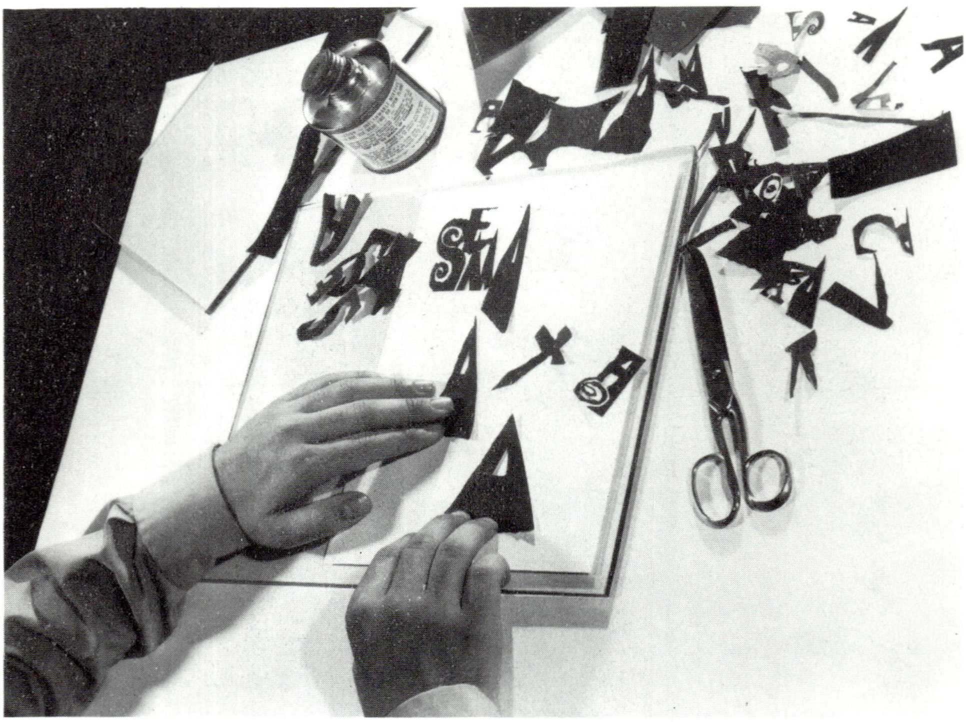

In order to create this kind of collage yourself, the best thing is to work on a piece of light white cardboard placed on a piece of glass. You then arrange and stick on the black paper shapes, fixing them on to the white cardboard with a dab of glue, and finally placing another piece of glass on top to form the sandwich which allows the whole to be photographed.

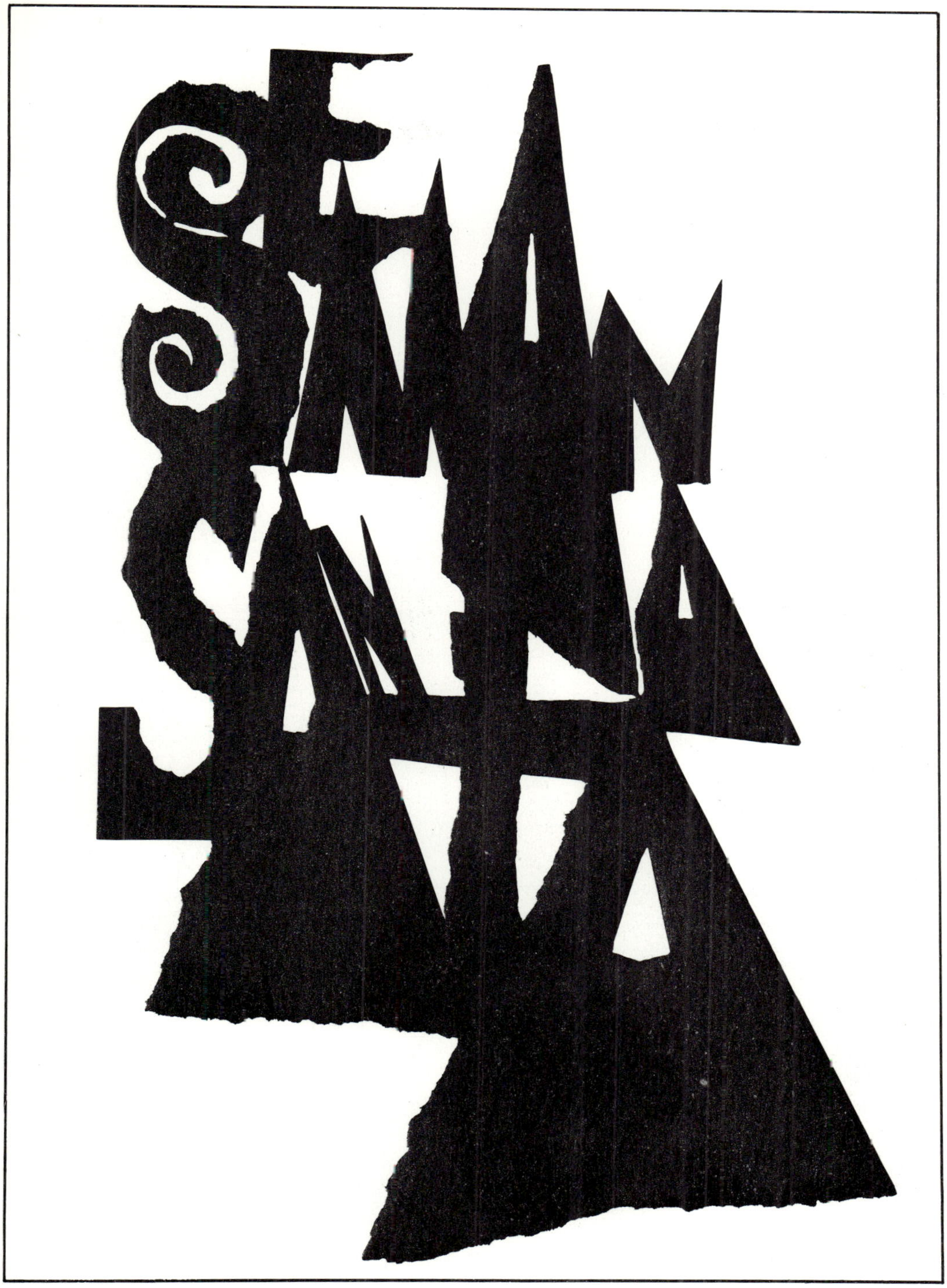

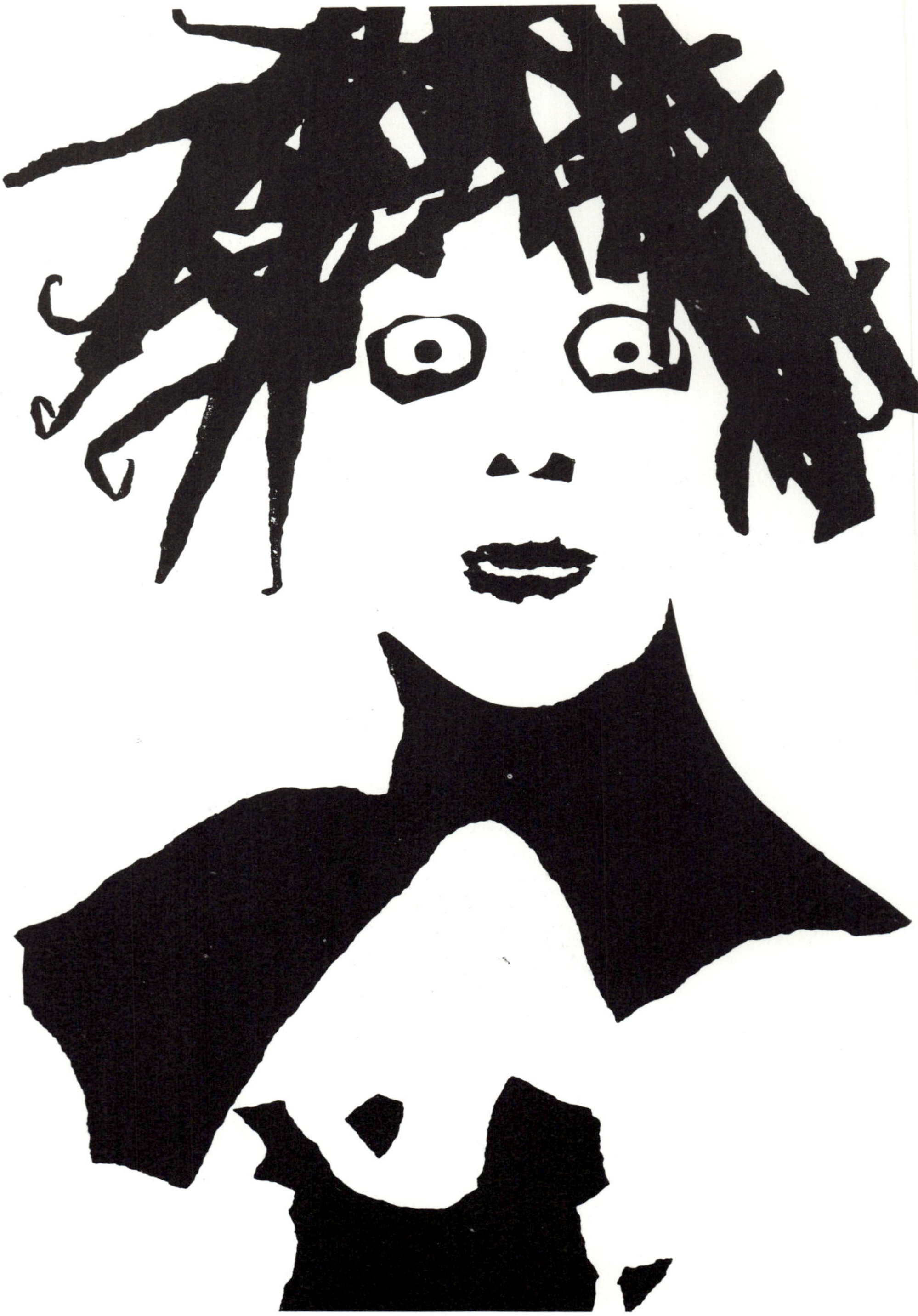

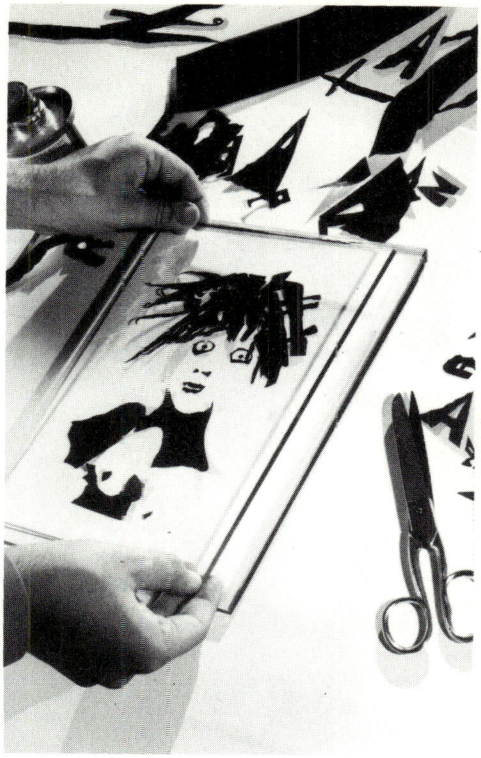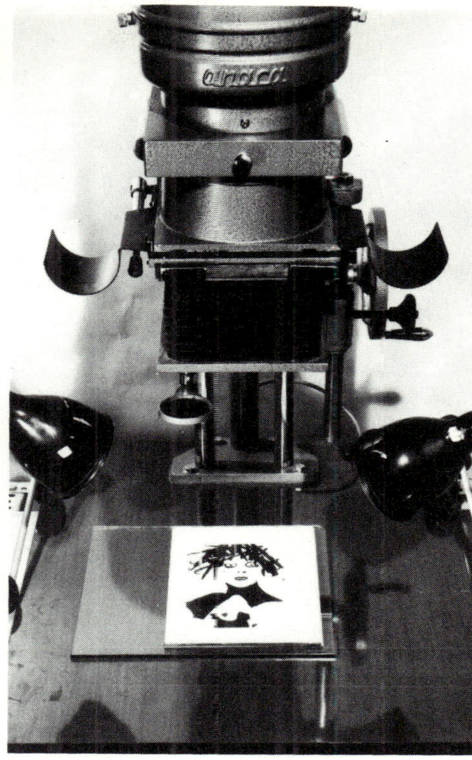

In order to make the picture of *The mad woman,* which is reproduced opposite, Plá Narbona did not trouble to stick down the bits of black paper shapes. He merely arranged the cut-out strips on a piece of white light cardboard and placed a piece of glass over the top, keeping the pieces in position. He transferred the sandwich to the photographic enlarger, as you can see above, to reproduce the picture and obtain a positive print to be made subsequently on photographic paper. This gives him absolute contrast.

thus formed is then taken to the enlarger and reproduced in the photographic laboratory. Here Plá Narbona reproduces the picture, thus obtaining a completely clear and contrasting copy (deep black with pure white) which enhances the picture.

In some cases, to create some of the pictures reproduced in these pages, Plá Narbona has not used glue at all; once he has put the pieces of paper in the right shape, hardly daring to breathe for fear of sending the lot flying, he carefully places a sheet of glass over the image and transfers the sandwich direct to the enlarger/reproducer.

Try and do something in this style of collage. Use the whitest piece of light cardboard you can find; not too big. Try shifting shapes around, and spend plenty of time composing, tearing out and building up. Stick the bits on lightly, and mount them between two pieces of glass. You'll see that it comes out very well. It was worth the effort to achieve a work of art, possibly a first-rate work of art.

PAINTING WITH A KNIFE

HOW TO SET ABOUT IT

A knife has a wooden handle and a flexible steel blade without a cutting edge and with a blunt triangular end. In some cases it has the characteristic form of a mason's trowel. (See below some of the most usual types.) **Definition of the knife**

As a medium for painting, the knife is an ideal tool for use as a brush when painting in oils or tempera. It provides an up-to-date work without much effort.

The knife was used as far back as the artists of the early centuries of the Christian era for painting in hot, coloured wax, the wax being mixed with distemper colours.

Rembrandt, painting in oils, was the first to use the knife and he used it for certain parts of his backgrounds and for clothing. But, in fact, it was Courbet, in the nineteenth century, who, after certain tests made by Delacroix with new techniques, used the knife as a medium for making pastes and mixing and applying the colours in the picture. **Short history**

Bear in mind the technique of Titian and Van Eyck, the first of whom used his fingers to plane down and embellish the colours

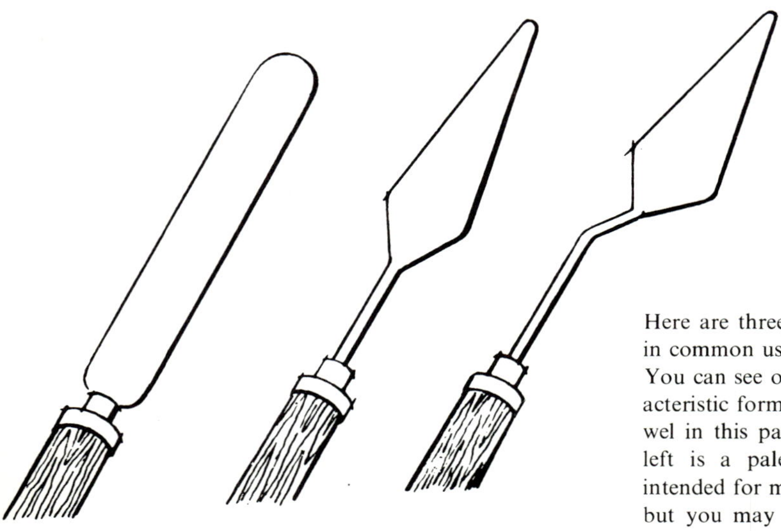

Here are three examples of knives in common use for painting in oil. You can see on the right the characteristic form of the mason's trowel in this painting knife. On the left is a palette knife which is intended for mixing on the palette, but you may try using it for applying paint.

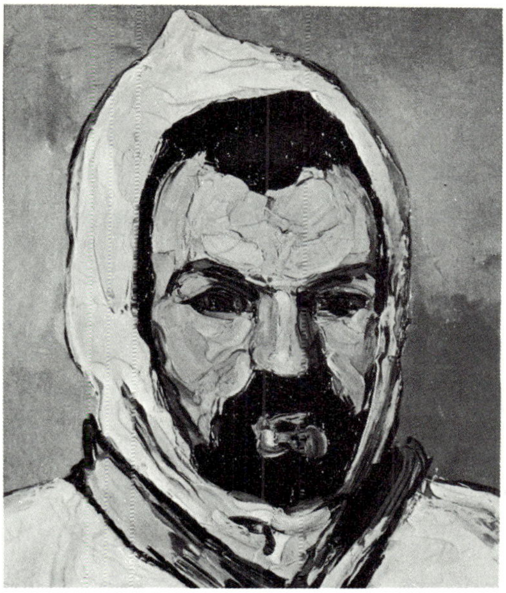

Towards the end of the last century, with the advent of Impressionism, many artists used the palette knife for painting in oils and often tried to bring the style of the picture up-to-date or modernize it, as in this portrait of *Uncle Dominique*, painted by Paul Cézanne in 1866. Here you can appreciate the vigour and synthesis of a finished work painted with the palette knife.

which had been recently applied. The second persisted with fine and oily layers, resembling the finish of Chinese and Japanese lacquers. If we think of these two artists we can better understand what the knife can supply: the lacquer, the smooth, brilliant and transparent finish.

Potential

When using a knife you can get mottled effects which look like brilliant and exotic marble. These are made into thick pastes of a texture which at times is similar to bas-relief. On the other hand, you can get plain and absolutely clear colours, thin and smooth, but which barely cover the grain of the canvas. This will give us a first glimpse of the potential, techniques and execution of painting with the knife.

As usual, practice is the best method for understanding and following these instructions.

Choose a model, arrange the canvas, prepare the colours (as you always do with oils, just as they come out of the tube on the palette), and take up the knife.

The first thing to do is to understand the process, handle the knife, make the paste, apply the colour and make a trial painting on your palette, on a piece of cardboard or on some other surface.

Arrangement of the colours

Now, arrange the oil colours on the palette in the usual order: from right to left, in the form of a circle round the edge of the palette. You begin with white followed by cadmium yellow, yellow ochre, cadmium red, rose madder, umber, viridian, cobalt blue, ultramarine and Prussian blue.

gathering up and piling up the paint when it spreads out too much and then whipping it up and blending it again, etc. (E).

When you are painting on a canvas you'll see how you can outline and draw shapes with a knife, especially one with a larger blade (F).

Two methods for painting with knife

You are now starting work on your picture. You can do it by mixing colours on the palette or mixing them on the canvas itself,

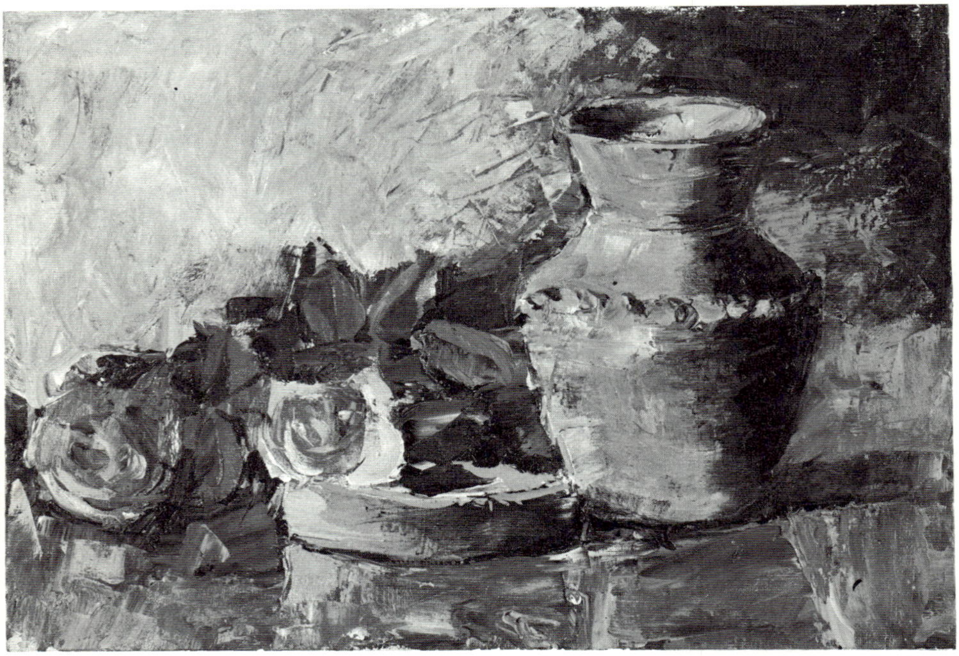

and you can paint over a sketch which has been previously toned in, or direct with the knife on the white, virgin canvas.

TWO EQUALLY GOOD METHODS

Painting over a thin layer

You can paint with the knife direct, or over a quick sketch made in very thin paint. The methods are described below:

Paint with the knife over a thin coat: the first stage will consist of painting in oils with plenty of turps, i.e., with very liquid colours which tinge the canvas, but are completely thin.

Over this first thin layer (with careful toning down or colouring which has been painted as well as possible), use your knife to mix either on the canvas or the palette; I would suggest you mix on the palette until you have had some experience of this technique.

Use the first application of paint on backgrounds and wide areas with your knife, leaving the final touches for more fiddly smaller areas.

Final retouching with brush

The final retouching should be done with a sable brush.

The difference between this method and the next is that the first method gives you a harmonized background. Painting each small part at the same time as constructing without drawing means difficulties and problems which you'll discover for yourself.

Painting direct on to the canvas with a knife: To obtain a more up-to-date style we recommend mixing the colours on the canvas itself, without the use of the palette.

First of all paint the larger areas, with no intention of giving the finishing touches or retouching in the later stages.

The more fragmented parts, with the most varied, small and complicated shapes, require a delicate treatment in the first phase which allows for emphasis in the later stages. In the smaller of these, it's best to apply colours which have been already mixed and prepared on the palette. But whenever you can, to produce a more modern work, attempt the direct method of mixing on the canvas itself, as though it were the palette.

It's important to remember that this system is really difficult, not to be advised for the inexperienced and quite out of the question for the amateur who hasn't complete mastery over the art of painting in oils with the brush.

In the last stage, when giving the final touches, it is perfectly all right to retouch and repaint with a sable brush, while trying not to destroy the smooth enamelled appearance which is so typical of knife work.

ALWAYS USE THE DIRECT METHOD

You'll know by now that knife painting always has to be done by the direct method, i.e., it has to be finished at a single sitting. So we'll exclude the large painting, the great subject and the laborious, large and finished work.

Cézanne used the knife for portraits, bur they weren't like the Ingres portraits, studied, detailed and most elaborate. Cézanne's were really rough sketches, almost drafts which he

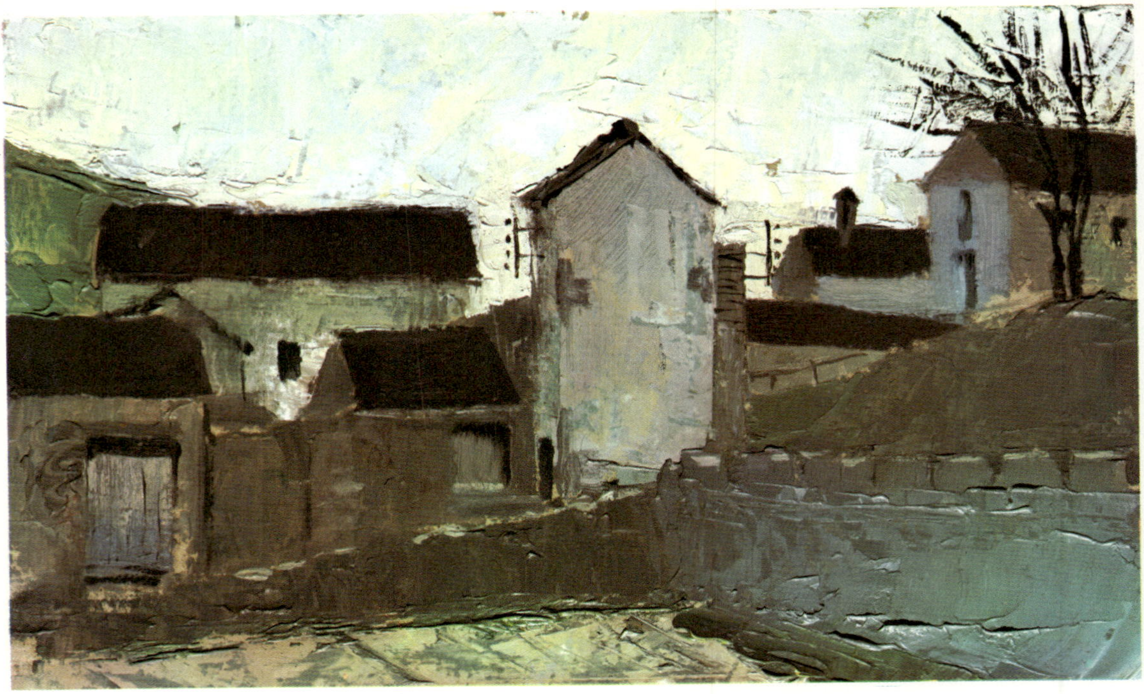

See above example of a landscape painted directly with a knife. Note the effects of this substance, the smooth richness of the sky compared with the rough rugged foreground.

---

constructed, with the edge and flat blade of the knife in a few moments, capturing the fleeting likeness of a human face, or an individual.

KNIFE EXECUTION... WITHOUT A KNIFE

If you are working in advertising and trying to paint an original, special and distinctive background: for a box, the wrapper for a pair of tights, for example, or for an advertisement background over which you will display an inscription or a logo, start like this:

Make a paste of tempera in a small cup and then pour it on to a piece of glass, which you'll use as a palette. Then take up the paint with a razor blade and rub the paint-covered edge of the blade on a piece of thick paper or light cardboard. You'll see what effects you can achieve — the mottled appearance and very special texture. Now have a good time, rotating the blade and scraping with it, taking up paint, "drawing" lines and light strokes on a dark-coloured background, moving and painting in zig-zags, superimposing curved shapes and so on.

MONOTYPE

Technique of the monotype process

FROM THEORY TO PRACTICE

YOU WILL NEED: OIL PAINTS AND BRUSHES, ETC; GOOD QUALITY LAID PAPER (OF INGRES TYPE). A PIECE OF THICK GLASS SLIGHTLY LARGER THAN THE PAINTING.

Take a piece of drawing paper, of a slightly spongy quality, Ingres-type for example. Paint with oils on a piece of glass equal in size to that of the sheet of drawing paper, and then put the drawing paper over the still soft paint on the glass. Now try to "print" the image, by transferring it from the glass to the paper and by pressing down with your hand or with a rag or some hard substance (a wooden spoon, for example).

Definition of monotype

Essentially, this is what the system known as monotype consists of. It is defined as "a single-printed example of an artistic work".

We'll go into more detail so that you can try it yourself and prove to yourself that it presents all kinds of ways to achieve a good painting.

The classical formula for achieving a monotype consists, as we have said, in printing a piece of drawing paper from a painting made on a piece of glass, i.e.

A single copy with a single impression

The classic monotype is a single copy produced from a single impression.

There is a somewhat freer technique — a monotype made by two successive impressions or, rather, by a single impression done on

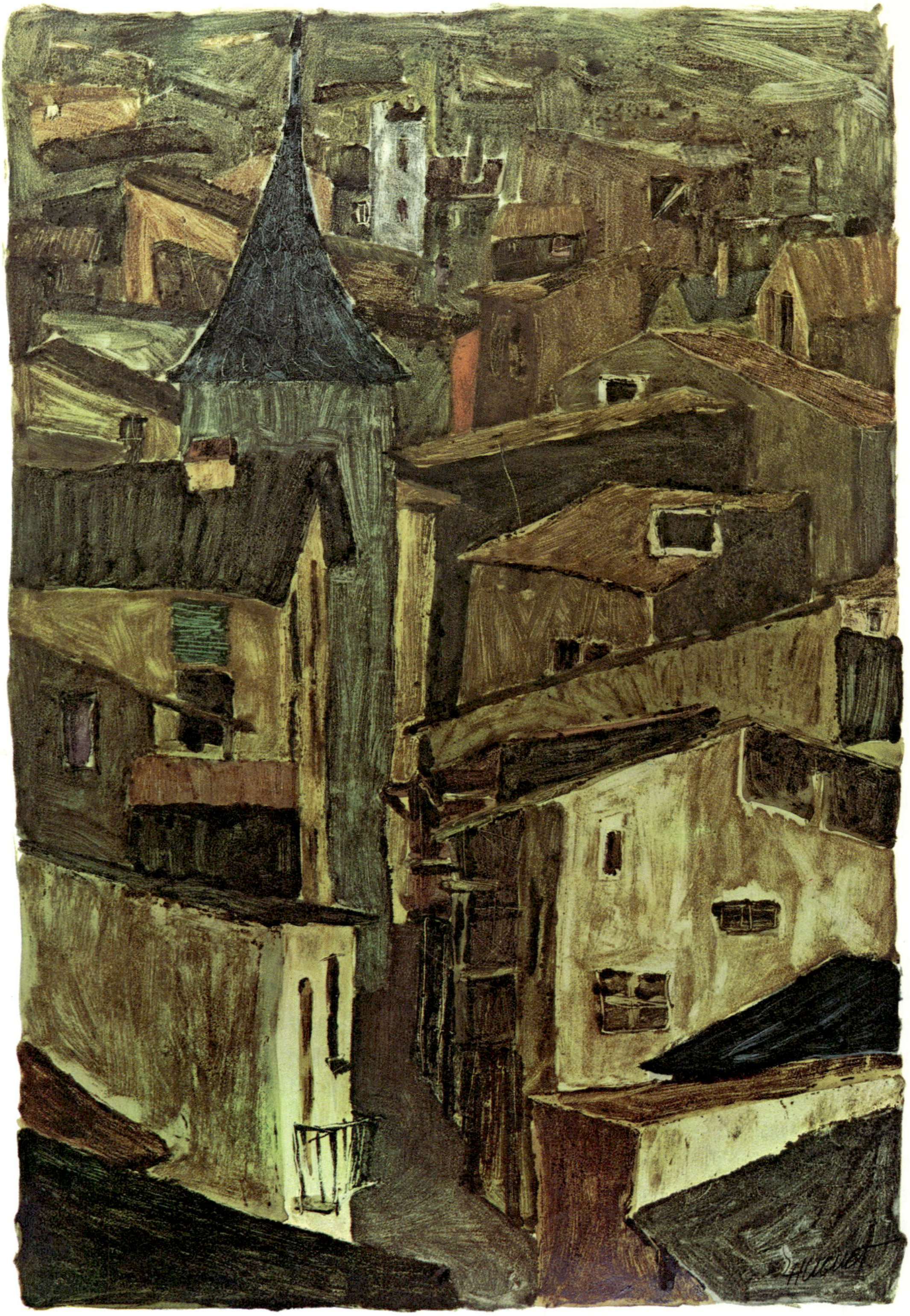

MONOTYPE

Technique of the monotype process

FROM THEORY TO PRACTICE

YOU WILL NEED: OIL PAINTS AND BRUSHES, ETC; GOOD QUALITY LAID PAPER (OF INGRES TYPE); A PIECE OF THICK GLASS SLIGHTLY LARGER THAN THE PAINTING.

Take a piece of drawing paper, of a slightly spongy quality, Ingres-type for example. Paint with oils on a piece of glass equal in size to that of the sheet of drawing paper, and then put the drawing paper over the still soft paint on the glass. Now try to "print" the image, by transferring it from the glass to the paper and by pressing down with your hand or with a rag or some hard substance (a wooden spoon, for example).

Definition of monotype

Essentially, this is what the system known as monotype consists of. It is defined as "a single-printed example of an artistic work".

We'll go into more detail so that you can try it yourself and prove to yourself that it presents all kinds of ways to achieve a good painting.

The classical formula for achieving a monotype consists, as we have said, in printing a piece of drawing paper from a painting made on a piece of glass, i.e.

A single copy with a single impression

The classic monotype is a single copy produced from a single impression.

There is a somewhat freer technique — a monotype made by two successive impressions or, rather, by a single impression done on a first layer. This process follows that of monotype, but has small variations from the classic method.

Printing on a layer of previous painting

Just try to print the monotype on a wash base. This provides a thicker colour base, which is finally expressed in a denser, more vigorous and energetic painting.

Dampen the paper first

Begin by dampening the drawing paper with water, using only a slightly dampened sponge. This allows one a damp impression as a basis on which the oil paints, transmitted by pressure, adhere better.

First, make a sketch

In practice, of course, you have to study the motif first and paint a small draft or sketch to enable you to see the whole. Reaching your goal is fairly easy when the motif's construction is a simple one with large areas, and when the colouring is adjusted to a range with a very marked tendency or dominant colour, and preferably a dense, greyish range.

Success may be handed to you on a plate if you are painting at home with all you need at hand. You can play fancy tricks which one wouldn't dare to perform outside, unprotected in the open air.

When the motif has been chosen, the subject carefully studied, and the sketch completed you follow these instructions:

1. Draw with a lead pencil

1. Starting from the previous sketch, draw the subject on the final paper, using a very soft pencil. This is just an outline, without shading.

2. Traced on paper

2. Then, using tracing paper of the same size as the paper for the final drawing, sketch the drawing mentioned in the previous paragraph. This stage is important; it has to serve as a guide for reproduction, helping you to paint on the reverse of the glass.

3. System for painting the picture in reverse

3. On a flat surface, a table for example, you need: a) a sheet of white paper; b) paper with your line drawing face downward on top, and c) the piece of glass, over both pieces of paper. This must be thick glass of a size slightly greater than the picture. Having arranged everything just so, thanks to the reflection of the white paper and to the transparency of the tracing paper, you'll see the drawing of the theme in reverse, so that by painting on the glass, we shall reverse the sides, but then, on impressing the painting of the glass on the final drawing paper, we shall again get a picture the right way round. If you know anything about the graphic arts, you'll know that it is logically assumed that, when you use an inverted block or picture the wrong way round, on being printed it becomes the right way round again (see illustrations).

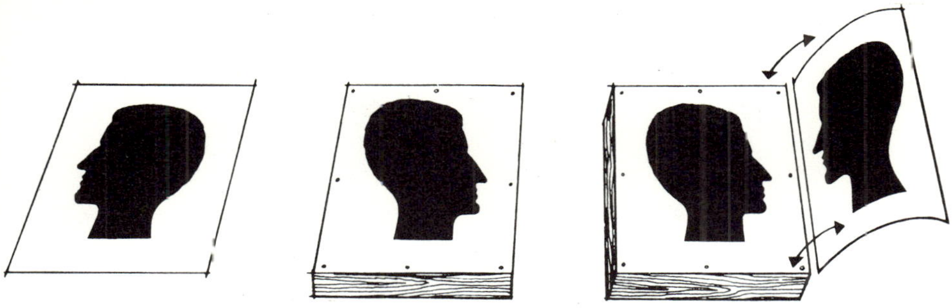

ORIGINAL PICTURE ENGRAVING IMPRESSION

Monotype, like every printing process involves painting in reverse in order to finish with a picture printed the right way round.

In order to get an absolute reproduction of your picture, it's as well to draw on the rough paper a few marks or little angles which coincide with the four corners of the final drawing paper, so that, in order to print and reprint, you have a guide which allows the first impression to be reproduced.

4. First coat in watercolours

4. Then begin the painting, working first of all on the final paper, in watercolours, "wet", with very delicate colours. These watercolours make the task easier because they dampen the paper, harmonize the colours and cover the paper with colour. This is in anticipation of the later impression with the glass and painting in oils, so that some areas should remain weak and with some lack of paint. This initial watercolouring should be meant only to stress the colour, and not be intended to draw the shapes. It should be used on a very extended plan and go far over the lines. It is the oils which are going to accomplish the shaping and limit the outlines and colours — the painting in oil applied on top of the glass.

5. Stretch the paint when painting the glass

5. For painting on the glass it's best to use broad-bladed brushes of a large size, with very thick paint. You'll need to stretch out the paint, leaving it in a much thinner layer. Try things out first, until you understand the technique.

6. Moisten the paper and make the impression

6. When the painting is over, the drawing paper is moistened — use only a little water — and carefully the paper is placed over the

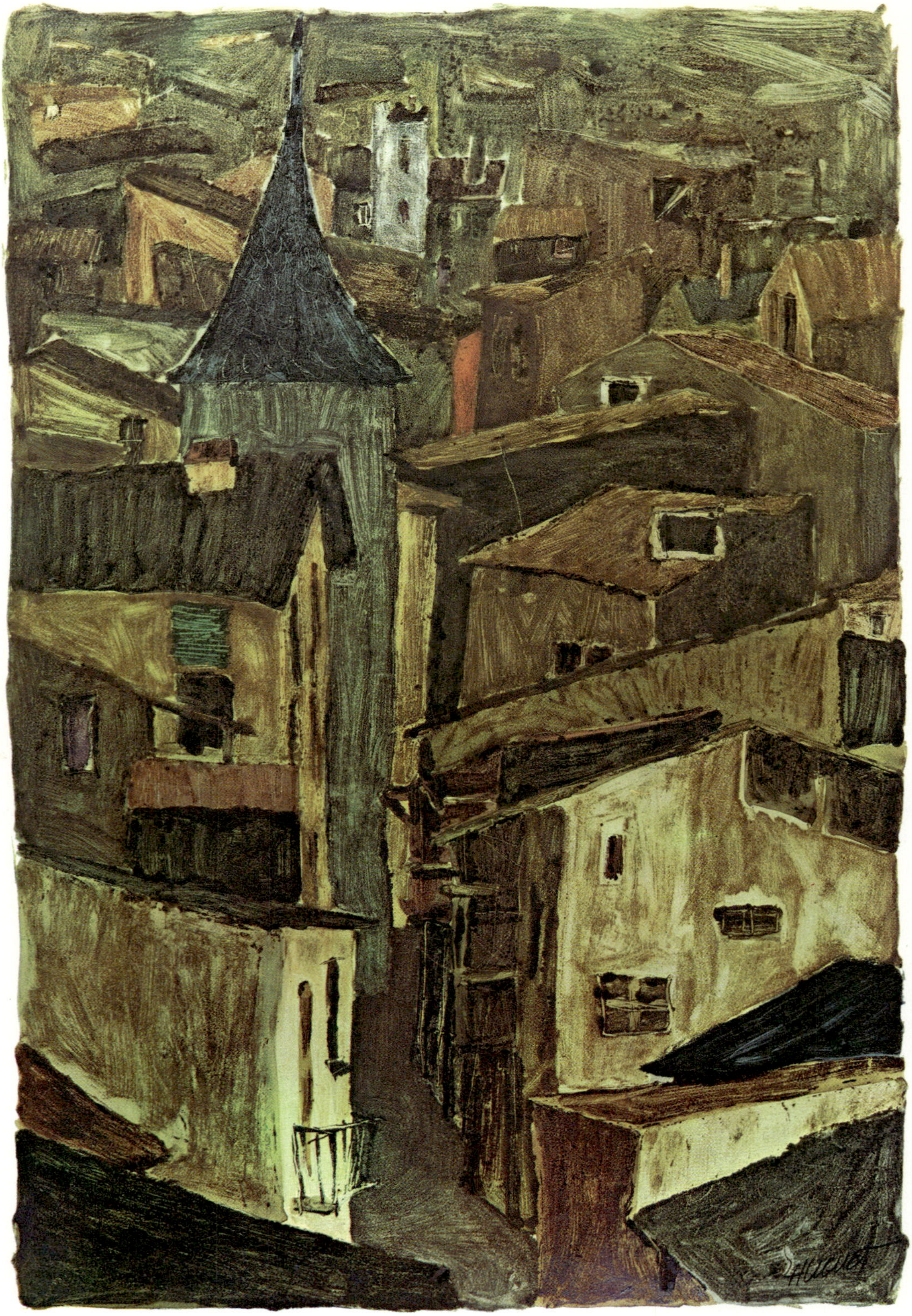

painting on the glass. Then begins the task of printing, using continuous hard pressure of the paper on the glass. The oil painting with its characteristic marks and that appearance of texture left by the hairs of the brush, will be printed on the drawing paper and give you a truly original finish.

While the impression is being made, it's as well to observe the effects produced by the pressure, noticing at which points the painting, on being compressed, runs the risk of spreading, staining and disfiguring the construction; also note at which points a greater pressure may be needed to achieve a greater intensity of colour or a certain special effect.

Final touches

Finally, when the paper has been pressed, and now it has been separated from the glass, some special retouching may be needed, or you may need to reinforce some stroke or line, hide some error, reinforce or intensify some small area, or even to trace some faint lines with the tip of the handle of the brush. Don't do much more than this. Here, as in every work of art, there is the danger of going too far, of touching up too much and so losing the freshness and spontaneity of the finish.

Try it out. It's great fun to do and it's a process which instructs, as well. I know someone who, through doing monotypes, ended up painting abstracts. And you will see that, when the colour flattens and spreads between glass and paper, the unexpected arises, with shapes and colours never imagined, an effect of colour and form which may be so abstract that it means nothing, but which speaks for itself in its essence of form and colour.

This brings the book to a close. While I was writing it and consulting the experts I realized that you, the reader, will get your own special effects. You'll find you get a tremendous sense of creativity by doing your own thing — don't get lost in the technique but produce something fresh and new each time and it will encourage you to experiment further.

First study the book and practise and you'll find ideas of your own, so you will be working and painting on your own behalf.

The facing page shows a monotype made by Enrique Huguet. You'll notice the marks of the brush strokes — characteristic of the monotype — which come from the marks and grooves left by the action of the brush when painting on glass. The brush has a very wide blade, bearing in mind the original size of this monotype (100 × 70 cm). Also note the range of colours used by Huguet, with siennas and khakis dominating the scene.